PARANORMAL SWANSEA AND GOWER

MARK REES

AMBERLEY

First published 2024

Amberley Publishing
The Hill, Stroud
Gloucestershire, GL5 4EP

www.amberley-books.com

British Library Cataloguing in Publication Data.
A catalogue record for this book is available from the British Library.

ISBN 978 1 3981 1487 6 (print)
ISBN 978 1 3981 1488 3 (ebook)

Typesetting by Hurix Digital, India.
Printed in Great Britain.

Contents

Introduction 5

Folklore and Superstition 7

- The Oxwich Water Horse 8
- The Bell and Candle Challenge 10
- Wicked Witchcraft 11
- The Devil Rides Out 13
- Beware the Little People 15
- The Curse of Pennard Castle 17
- Flight of the Swan-maiden 20
- Arthur's Stone 20

Haunted History 23

- Rhossili Bay 24
- Oystermouth Castle 27
- The Demon House 29
- The Red Lady of Paviland 30
- Port Eynon Salt House 33
- Whiteford Sands 35
- Mumbles Lighthouse 38
- Rejected by the Sea 40

Age of Copperopolis 41

- Swansea Séances 42
- The Graveyard Ghost 44
- Uncanny Wraith of a Murderer 45
- Superstitious Miners 46
- A Ghost to Rival Hamlet's Father 47
- Paranormal Hoaxers 49
- The Caswell Ghost 50
- Spring-heeled Swansea Jack 52

Modern-day Terrors 55
- Rhondda Street Poltergeist 55
- Jersey Lil 58
- Phantoms of Penllergare 59
- Blasts from the Past 62
- The Haunted Road 63
- The Bed-flipping Phantom 65
- The Reverend's Haunted House 65
- The White Lady of Pwlldu Bay 66

Cultural Curiosities 68
- Swansea Grand Theatre 69
- Swansea Museum 73
- Wind Street and Swansea Castle 76
- 1940s Swansea Bay 80
- Spooky SA1 82
- Welcome to Town 84
- Gower Heritage Centre 86
- The Haunts of Dylan Thomas 89

Bibliography 94
Acknowledgements 95
About the Author 96

Introduction

My ghost hunting career, as it were, began in Swansea many years ago. It was while working as a journalist in the city that I started publishing reports from such 'most haunted' places as Oystermouth Castle, Gower Heritage Centre, and Swansea Grand Theatre. Not simply researching and writing about these places – I rolled up my sleeves and went investigating the hard way. When most sensible people were tucked up in bed, I was sitting in cold, empty buildings, often without even the most basic of modern conveniences, trying to warm myself with a cup of coffee and hoping beyond hope that something – anything – would happen.

While this might sound like some strange form of self-inflicted punishment, I assure you it was not. As any committed paranormal investigator will tell you, it's the tiredness, discomfort, disappointment, and at times sheer mind-numbing futility of it all that makes it worthwhile. Because when something – anything – does happen, those seemingly endless hours beforehand disappear in an instant.

I was rarely alone on these vigils and was lucky enough to join many enthusiastic teams and researchers along the way. I met experts, enthusiasts, historians, and mediums, and despite their often-opposing personal beliefs, they all shared one thing in common: a passion for the paranormal. It might be a cliché, but it's true; the individuals who make up the paranormal community are some of the friendliest people you could ever wish to meet, many of whom I now consider very good friends.

The accounts in this book, some of which draw upon those early investigations, have been divided into five sections that will take you on a centuries-spanning voyage through the paranormal activity reported in the city and county of Swansea. As you will discover, they evolve with time and become what some might describe as more 'believable' with each chapter. We begin with the earliest and most fantastical stories of witches, devils, and fairy folk, and this is an area where Gower truly excels. We then move on to the more historical tales of smugglers and shipwrecks along Swansea Bay, before reaching the 'golden age' of ghosts, the Victorian era. The last two chapters bring things up to date with tales of twentieth-century apparitions and the spirits that haunt our cultural hotspots, because no self-respecting city is complete without a haunted theatre or two.

The final entry is reserved for a figure who haunts Swansea more than any other, the poet Dylan Thomas. Like myself, Dylan also began his writing career in Swansea and wrote for the local newspaper, although sadly that is where our literary similarities start and end. His words cast a long shadow over the streets he once walked, and he famously described his hometown as an 'ugly, lovely town'. This characteristically contradictory description could also be applied to its ghostly inhabitants, because for every poltergeist hellbent on causing destruction, there's a sensitive soul who just wants to rest in peace.

As I put the finishing touches to this book it really does feel like my journey into the ghosts and folklore of Wales has come full circle, back to where it all began, and I'd like to thank everyone who has joined me for the ride. To quote Dylan: 'Swansea is still the best place.'

Mark Rees, 2024

Folklore and Superstition

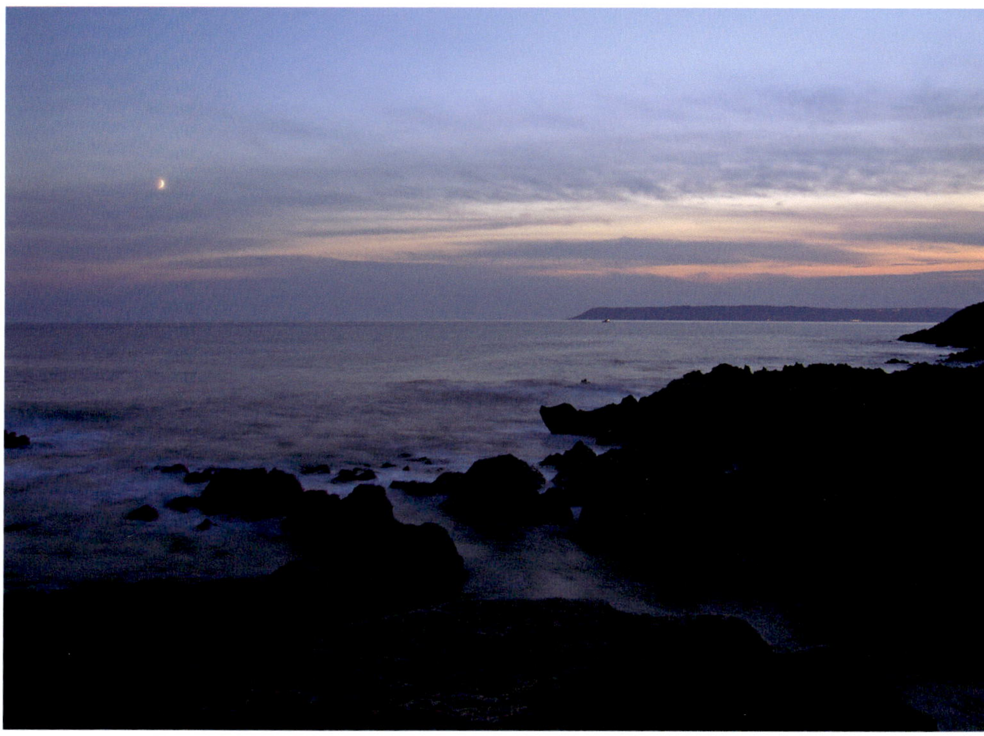

When the sun sets, the creatures of lore emerge. (© Gene Selkov, Flickr, CC BY 2.0)

Wales is a country steeped in myths and legends. From the snow-capped mountains of the north to the mystical coasts in the west, it is a land of Arthurian heroes, fire-breathing dragons, stargazing giants, and life-saving mermaids. The supernatural beings that stalk the shadows of Swansea and Gower might not be as fantastical as those found in the surrounding counties, but they are no less fascinating – or dangerous – as a result. Folklore speaks of demons and witches emerging at night, and even the birds and animals can't be trusted. In Gower, for example, a black fox indicated death or misfortune for the poor farmers on whose lands they appeared, while the sound of the woodpecker represented the tormented spirit of a woodman doomed to haunt the woods for neglecting his wife and children to starvation. In this opening chapter, we begin our quest for the paranormal with a selection of centuries-old tales that are still spoken of in hushed tones today.

The Oxwich Water Horse

The Church of St Illtyd has a distinctive square churchyard that, if the stories are to be believed, welcomes a rather unusual nighttime visitor. Overlooking the crashing waves of Oxwich Bay, the church is a Grade II* listed building that dates mainly from the twelfth century but stands on the site of much older churches. In the late Victorian age, the Revd John David Davies recalled how his older brother, when a boy of around thirteen years old, was fishing with their father in the sea below. It was gone midnight by the time they called it a day, and as they made their way back up the winding path towards the rectory, he had the strangest sensation of being followed. He looked back and saw 'a white horse walking on its hind legs' and watched in amazement as it drifted along towards the church. He alerted his father and they both saw it cross the stile by the gate and enter the grounds before disappearing. It has been suggested that it vanished into a well and that it might have been the Welsh water horse (ceffyl dŵr) of folklore. Whatever it was, the father was in no mood to investigate, and quickly hurried his son home. He did not speak of the affair again, and the reverend, who only wrote of the events after his father's death, implied that he knew more about the mystery than he dared admit. Nearly a century later, somebody else had a similar experience, and this time they were more than happy to talk about it. In the 1960s, the press reported that an older member of the community with 'unquestionable integrity' had been in the same churchyard at around midnight and saw a white form 'gliding over the grave tops'.

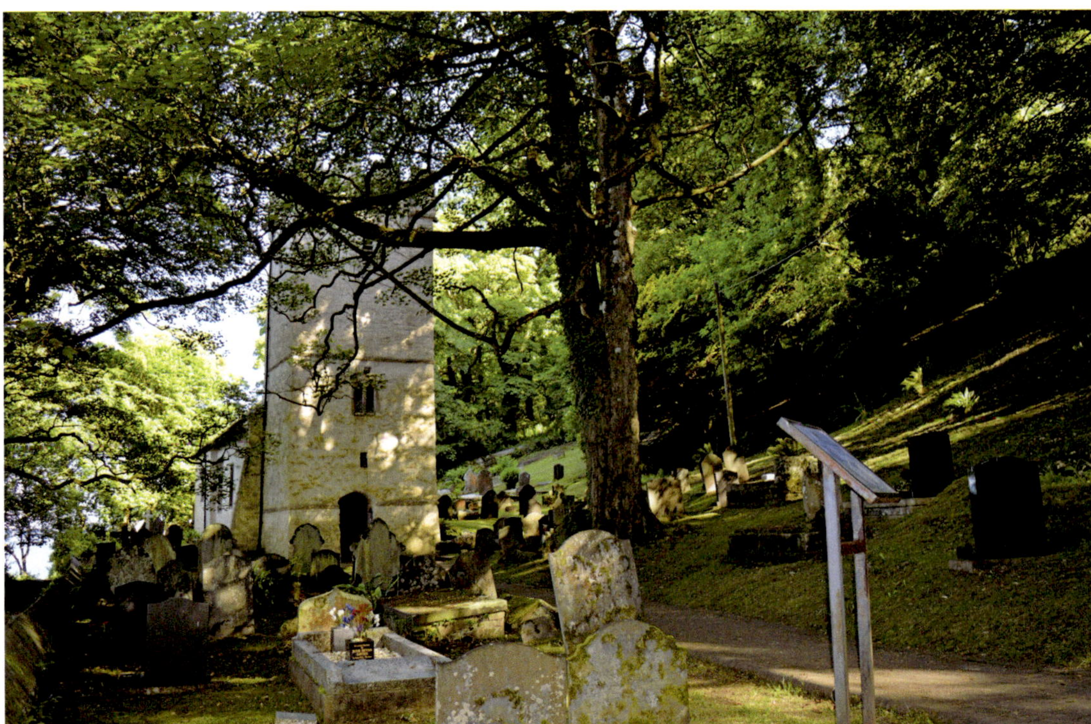

St Illtyd, Oxwich. (© Philip Pankhurst, CC BY-SA 2.0)

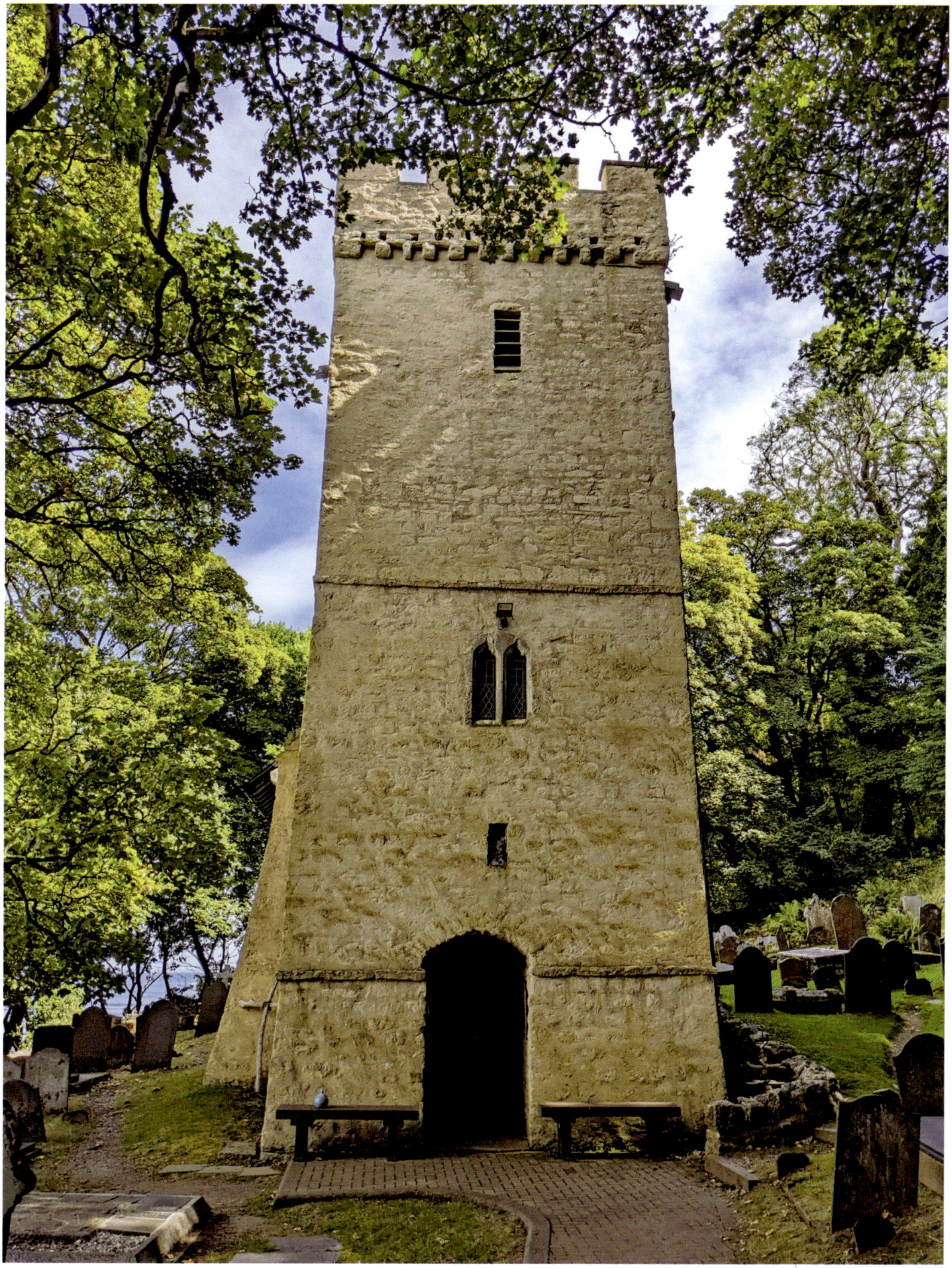

St Illtyd, Oxwich. (© The Wub, CC BY-SA 4.0)

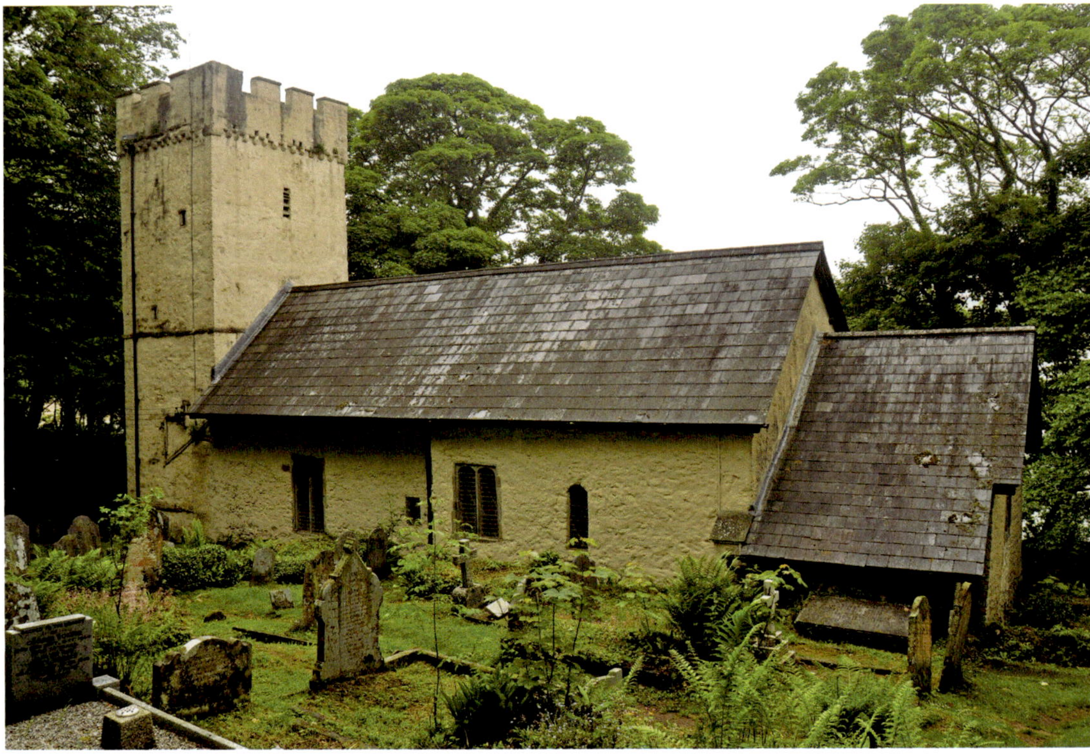

St Illtyd, Oxwich. (© Nilfanion, CC BY-SA 4.0)

The Bell and Candle Challenge

A strange phenomenon that can be observed on Caswell Bay has its origins in an even stranger tale concerning the Old Manor House in Bishopston. It was home to the rector who, despite living alone, shared it with an uninvited guest, the spirit of a white lady who was far from a quiet housemate. She would smash the crockery, topple the sideboard, and stomp around the unused rooms and staircase. Whenever the noise and destruction got too much for the priest he would flee to the safety of a nearby house, but if anyone ever accompanied him back they never witnessed a thing. As a result, the community considered him to be more eccentric than haunted, and when he needed help, he was forced to turn to a rather unconventional source: the local wise woman. She advised him to try the bell and candle challenge, a rather intricate and risky religious procedure much like the bell, book and candle ceremony used for excommunication. It required gathering twelve clerics to stand around his kitchen table in darkness with a lit candle and bell before them. At the stroke of midnight, the ghost would be summoned and challenged to blow out all the candles within a minute. Very much an all-or-nothing game, if the spirit was successful, they were free to haunt the house forevermore; but if they failed, they were sentenced to an endless task that would occupy them for eternity.

The rector followed the steps exactly, and as the witching hour approached, he heard the familiar sounds of the spirit's approach. When she appeared in the kitchen

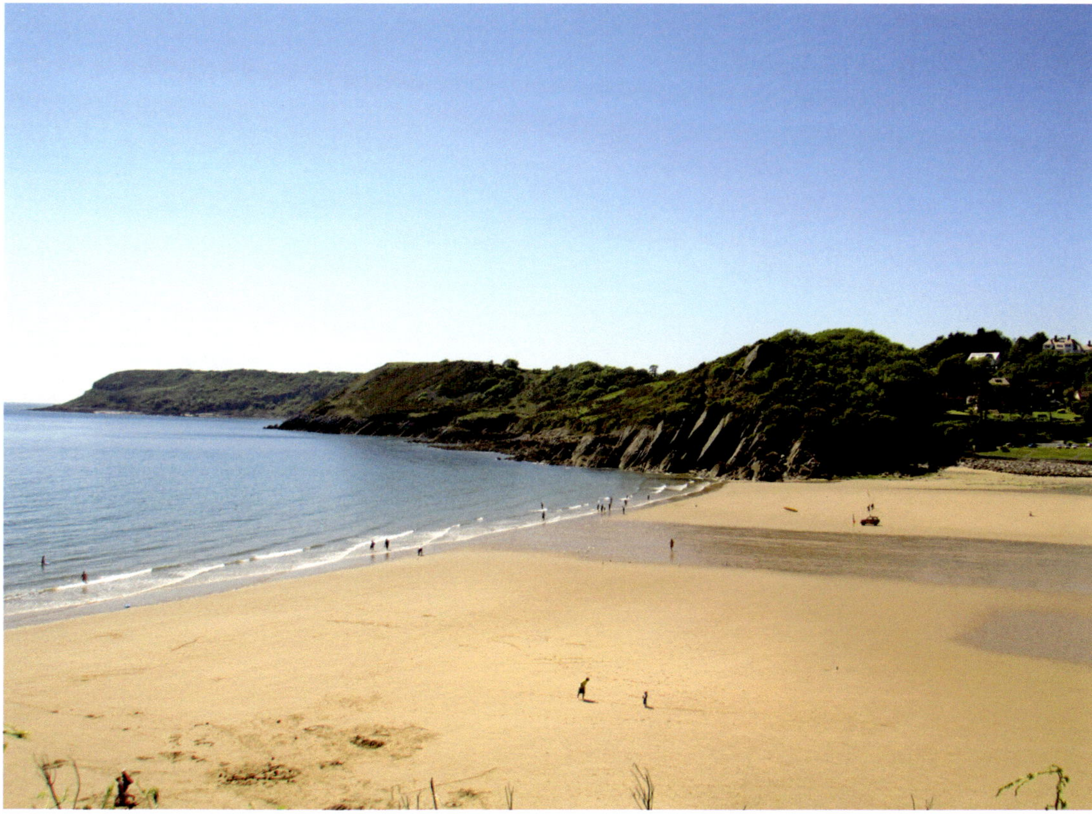

Caswell Bay. (© Tom Bastin, Flickr, CC BY 2.0)

and cast her eyes on the candles she was obliged to participate in the game, and with a face like thunder angrily blew out the first candle. The minute had begun, and the clerics suddenly emerged from the shadows and picked up their bells. Their thunderous clanging shook the spook into indecision, and while she recovered to blow out a few more, at the end of the sixty seconds seven still burned. The dejected spirit waited to discover her fate, and the holy men sentenced her in unison. She was instructed to build a sandcastle below high water on Caswell Bay that could survive three days and three nights of the tide, a chore she had little chance of ever completing. She left the house, the room was bricked up, and the haunting was over.

Today, if you watch over Caswell Bay as the tide comes in, you might notice the sand making unnatural shapes, as if being disturbed by some invisible presence. It is accompanied by a high-pitched whistling noise that whizzes past the ear. This is the sound of the white lady retreating from the approaching water to the nearby woods to watch her handiwork being destroyed once more.

Wicked Witchcraft

Gower has long been a haven for practitioners of witchcraft. These wise men and women, as they were known, were well versed in the magical arts, and their secret

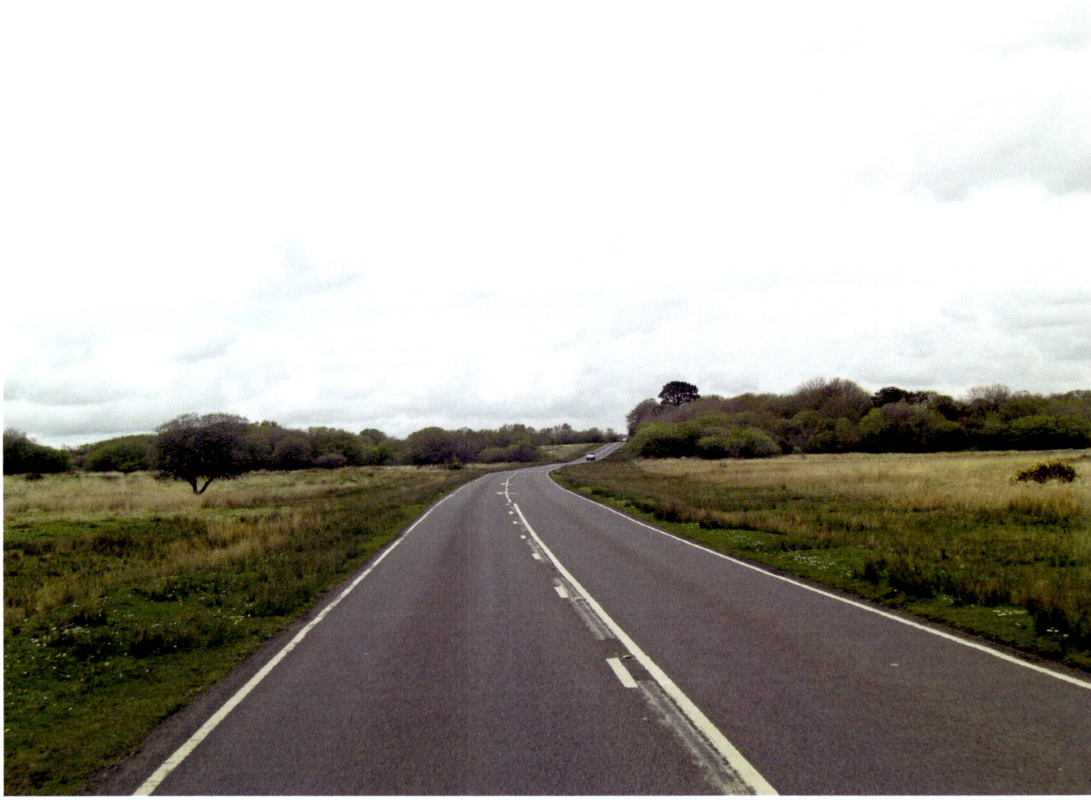

Fairwood Common. (© Stuart Logan, CC BY-SA 2.0)

knowledge, passed down through the generations, allowed them to provide many useful services. From healing the sick to predicting the future, they were valued members of the community who, in times of crisis, could conjure up some incredibly powerful spells. For example, they could raise a storm by making a small perforation in an eggshell, sucking out the yolk, and then capturing bad weather inside. By sealing the eggshell with shoemaker's wax, the storm could be released when needed by smashing the egg on a stone.

Not all of these 'witches', however, were believed to use their powers for good, and the most notorious woman to be accused of practising dark magic was Old Moll. She shunned society and lived a nocturnal existence as a hermit, possibly in a cave near Brandy Cove, and would stalk Fairwood Common after the shades of night had fallen. Simply crossing her path was bad luck, and she was blamed for any misfortune that might occur afterwards, from crops failing to livestock dying. One child who was foolish enough to make fun of her face was blighted with nightmares. The locals tried to drive her away with sticks and stones, but there was little chance of them hurting her as she had the ability to transform into a hare and make a quick exit. Nevertheless, the people of Gower were determined to rid themselves of Old Moll, and believing that silver could defeat witchcraft, they gathered anything silver they owned and melted it down to make bullets. When she was next seen gathering firewood they gave chase, and when she transformed into a hare they began to shoot. The animal was hit in the leg and left a trail of blood, at the end of which they found the witch in human form cowering under her dark cloak. She was not seen in Gower again, but a cloaked figure with a limp is still said to haunt the historic county of Glamorgan.

The Devil Rides Out

In days gone by, the Devil was an ever-present threat for the God-fearing people of Wales. In Llangyfelach, for example, the Evil One tried to steal the tower from the church, but only succeeded in detaching it from the main building. He was stopped in his tracks by Cyfelach, the saint who lends his name to the village. Sailors would speak of how Satan sailed around Wales gathering souls in a three-masted ship made from wood cut in Hell, and it was another Welsh saint – St David in some versions of the tale, St Donat in others – who ended this unholy harvesting by piercing the hull with his holy spear. Old Nick was forced to swim away, and his wrecked ship crashed ashore on the Gower coast where a giant made a toothpick of the mast and a handkerchief of the mainsail.

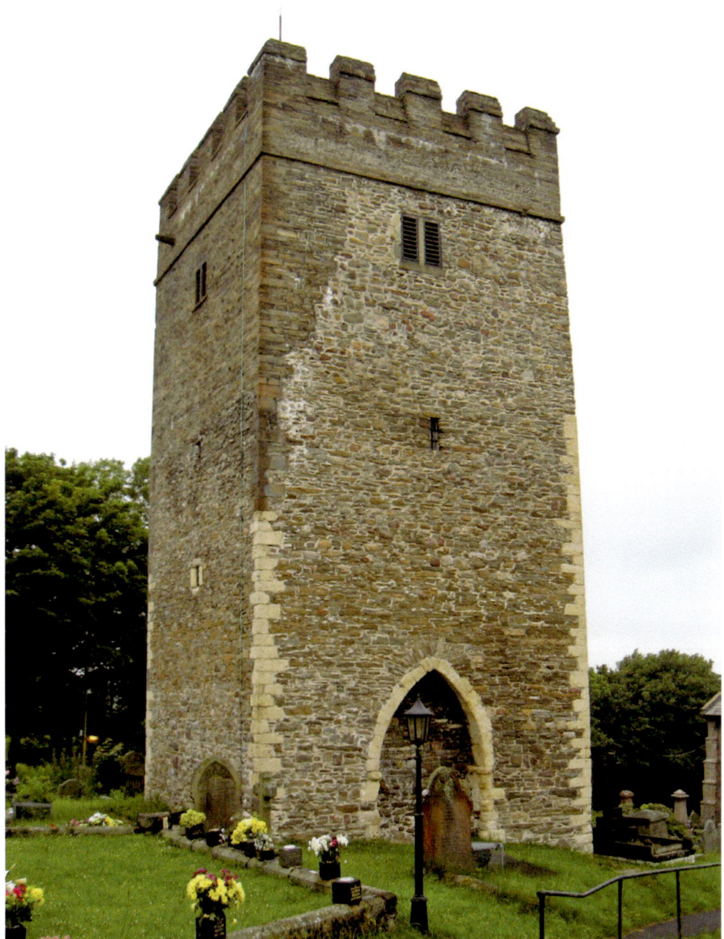

The tower at St David and Cyfelach, Llangyfelach. (© Chris Andrews, CC BY-SA 2.0)

In the nineteenth century, a tale was recorded in which a 'fair and gentle maiden' living in Gower would sneak off during the summer months for long walks with a mysterious lover. Nobody knew where she went or with who, only that she returned afterwards 'radiant with joy'. One moonlit night, a curious friend followed her to a widespread oak where, despite appearing to be alone, she began whispering sweet nothings under the tree – was she talking to herself? A sense of dread swept over them, and they rushed home to tell the household. They questioned her when she returned, but she insisted there was nothing to worry about and that her lover was a perfect gentleman. The next night they all followed her, and after witnessing a repeat performance were convinced that she'd been tempted by the 'Spirit of Darkness'. This time they insisted that she stop these late-night rendezvous, and while the girl understood their concerns, she could not resist the overpowering urge to return. She did, however, take her Bible with her for protection, and as she approached the tree the weather seemed to confirm their suspicions. Dark clouds swept across the sky and blocked the light from the moon, only for a sudden flash of lightning to briefly illuminate the world. In that instant she saw a tell-tale sign that he was no ordinary man: a horrible cloven hoof. With a loud scream she fled, and the valley screamed with her. Demonic howls echoed all around, thunder and lightning shook the hills, and a ferocious whirlwind ripped ancient trees from the ground. The next morning the household awoke to find a scene of devastation outside, in the centre of which was a huge stone. The vengeful demon, in his fury, had torn it from the hillside and flung it at the maiden who was never seen again. If you know where to look, you might find 'Demon's Rock' in Gower today.

In another tale, a blacksmith was working at night when a peculiar stranger entered his forge. They asked why he was hammering away at such an hour, and the blacksmith explained that he had an important commission. A master mariner

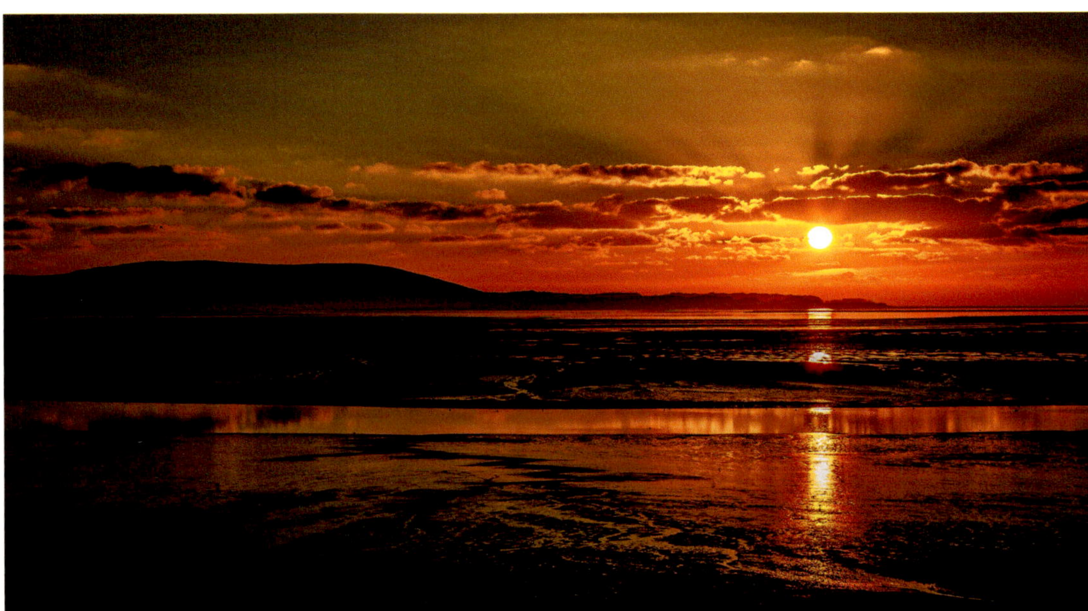

When the sun sets on Gower, the Devil emerges. (© David Potter, Flickr, CC BY-ND 2.0)

needed a chain forged that was strong enough to hold a ship, so strong it could hold even the devil himself, and when the visitor heard this he laughed and asked if he really believed he could create such a chain. The blacksmith assured him that he could, but the stranger boasted that he was strong enough to break any chain made by man and would return in a week to prove it. Seven days later he reappeared as promised, and when the blacksmith asked what his name was, he replied that, while he had many names, as he had arrived to help in the nick of time, he could call him Nicholas. The blacksmith wrapped the chain around Nicholas's waist and called his four apprentices to hold the other end. Nicholas, clearly amused at the idea that these mortals believed they could outmuscle him in a game of tug-of-war, slowly but surely walked backwards out of the door, dragging the men with him. When he grew tired of toying with them, he decided to end the contest with a sudden yank of the chain. This was exactly the moment the four men had been waiting for, and they all loosened their hold together. Nicholas was sent flying backwards towards a deep pool with an old winch in the middle that he had been edging closer to. As he hit the water it hissed like a boiling cauldron, and that was the last time Nicholas was seen in that part of Gower.

In Llanrhidian, meanwhile, a priest awoke from a vivid dream in which he had followed a set of cloven footprints to a nearby cove. Inside the cove he heard the faint sound of a Welsh lullaby and saw a vast hoard of gold illuminated by a flickering lantern. He took this to be a revelation, and despite the obvious warning sign that the footprints probably didn't belong to anyone on the side of God, that evening he went in search of the loot accompanied by a servant carrying a harp. When they arrived at the location the servant played the same melody heard in the dream, and with that the entrance began to open. They could see the gold inside and rushed in to claim it, but when the music stopped the entrance started closing behind them. They were never seen again, and it is said that if you walk past the right cove when the air is still you can still hear that haunting tune drifting on the wind.

Beware the Little People

Ask someone to describe a fairy and there's a pretty good chance they'll paint a picture of a petite, winged, human-like creature that dances around the bottom of the garden or stars in Disney films. But this wasn't always the case, and in days gone by much of the paranormal activity now blamed on poltergeists and demons, from the destruction of property to unexplainable mishaps, was considered the work of the fair folk.

In Wales, fairies are popularly known as *y tylwyth teg* (the fair family) but, just like accents, vary from place to place. A variety unique to Gower are the verry volk, who enjoy music and dancing in the moonlight. They perform good deeds and are generally welcoming, but they can also be mischievous, and if crossed their vengeance is deadly. An example of their dual nature can be found in the tale of an old woman in Llanmadoc, who they regularly surprised with gifts of money but stopped suddenly when she broke their golden rule and told someone of their visits. They also gave her son Willie John a magical sieve that could brew unlimited amounts of super-strength ale, but this also came to a halt thanks to his mother's loose tongue. Another story recalls how a trader from Gower was on his way to Swansea Market to sell his produce, but the verry volk insisted he stop and dance with them for a while. He did as they asked and, despite arriving late, had an unexpectedly profitable day.

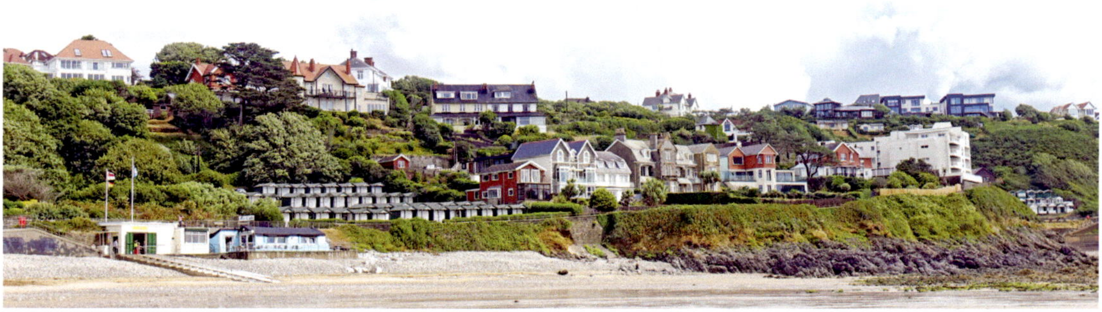

A view of Langland Bay, Newton. (© Tiia Monto, CC BY-SA 3.0)

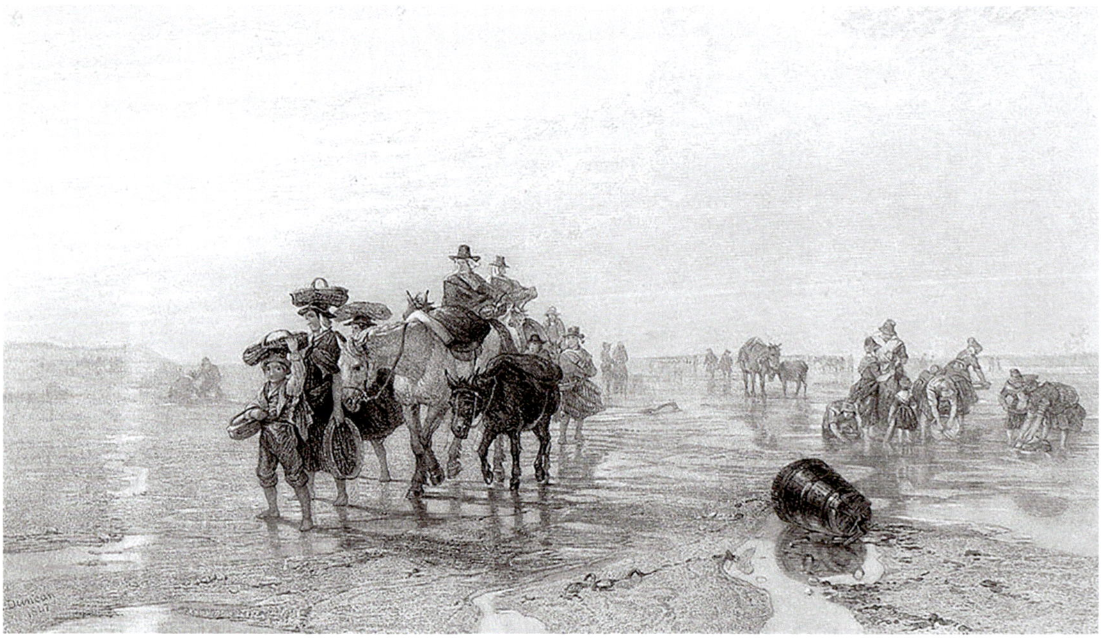

Cockle gatherers on the Llanrhidian Sands, who would sell their produce at Swansea Market (1849).

A far stranger encounter took place on Eynonsford Farm, a lonely longhouse near Reynoldson. The farmer was awoken one night by the sound of music in his cow shed, and when he peered inside, he found it filled with 'little beings' swarming all over his prized ox. Frozen in terror, he could only watch as they stopped dancing and started slaughtering, eating the animal in a frenzy until there was nothing but skin and bones. Afterwards, they reassembled the skeleton, stretched the hide back over it, and the ox magically returned to life. Under normal circumstances the farmer would have dismissed the entire affair as a bad dream, but there was one detail he could not dispute. In their ravenous feasting they had carelessly thrown the bones about the shed, and when it came to putting them back together again could not find a small leg bone. It was later discovered by the farmer, and from that day forth, the ox had a lameness in that leg.

Another small magical creature more commonly associated with Cornwall and Devon has been sighted in Newton. In the late nineteenth century, a woman claimed that pixies were dancing on the back of her father's grey mare as she prepared it to carry produce to Swansea Market. She believed these 'tiny men' were spirits that appeared early in the morning and were to blame for any bad luck that befell the cattle.

The Curse of Pennard Castle

Pennard Castle, according to folklore, is guarded by one of Wales's most terrifying death omens: the Gwrach y Rhibyn. This witch-like figure, known as the 'hag of the mist' in English, shares similarities with the Irish banshee, and is more harpy than human. She flies through the night sky on leathery wings, serving as a warning to those she visits that the end is nigh. According to a popular legend, anyone who spends the night in Pennard Castle will be bewitched by the Gwrach, and one young man from Carmarthen discovered this the hard way when a ghost-like figure attacked him and left him for dead. He was found bloody and bruised the next day and spoke of how a witch had clawed and pecked at him like a frenzied bird of prey. He considered himself lucky to be alive at the time, but soon discovered he had not escaped the Gwrach's curse, and from that day forth was 'bewitched' to live out his life as a 'lunatic'.

History tells us that the castle was originally built in stone for the powerful Braose family at the turn of the thirteenth and fourteenth centuries. Legend, however, tells us that it sprang up in a single night at the behest of a particularly impatient Norman lord who employed a sorcerer instead of builders. This lord was a nasty piece of work, as were those he associated with, and when they all gathered at the castle for his daughter's wedding the celebrations descended into a scene of bacchanalian revelry. When the festivities were interrupted by strange lights in the woods outside, the lord gathered a party to go and put an end to the disturbance. They discovered that the source of the illuminations was the verry volk, the Gower fairy folk, who were also celebrating the princess's big day and assumed the lord's visit was a cordial one to thank them for honouring the occasion. But the lord, in his drunken stupor, mistook their merriment as a sign of aggression, and ordered his men to attack. The verry volk were defenceless and a bloodbath ensued, with very few surviving besides the queen. She stared into the eyes of the aggressor and cursed him with a single word: 'coward!' The next day, nursing a hangover, the lord watched with growing apprehension as dark clouds gathered in the sky. The waves became violent in the sea, a sandstorm whipped the battlements, and a terrifying screaming noise echoed throughout the castle. They instinctively knew it was the cry of the Gwrach y Rhibyn, and as her shriek reached fever pitch, sand flew over the ocean from Ireland and smothered the castle and everyone inside.

The castle was indeed abandoned due to encroaching sand, although whether this was the result of a vengeful curse or not is open to debate, and the Gwrach's wailing cry is still heard on strong westerly gales by those who haunt the area today – golfers. Sometimes, legend and reality meet, and one man who grew up in Gower had his own 'paranormal experience' at the castle. In 1998, Gregg Stockdale and a group of friends dared each other to walk around the local haunted locations on Halloween. They visited spooky landmarks while telling ghost stories, and bravely timed their tour to arrive at the castle at midnight. Gregg recalls: 'In true cliché fashion, a thick fog rolled in from the sea as we sat with the castle behind us. The storyteller of the group tapped

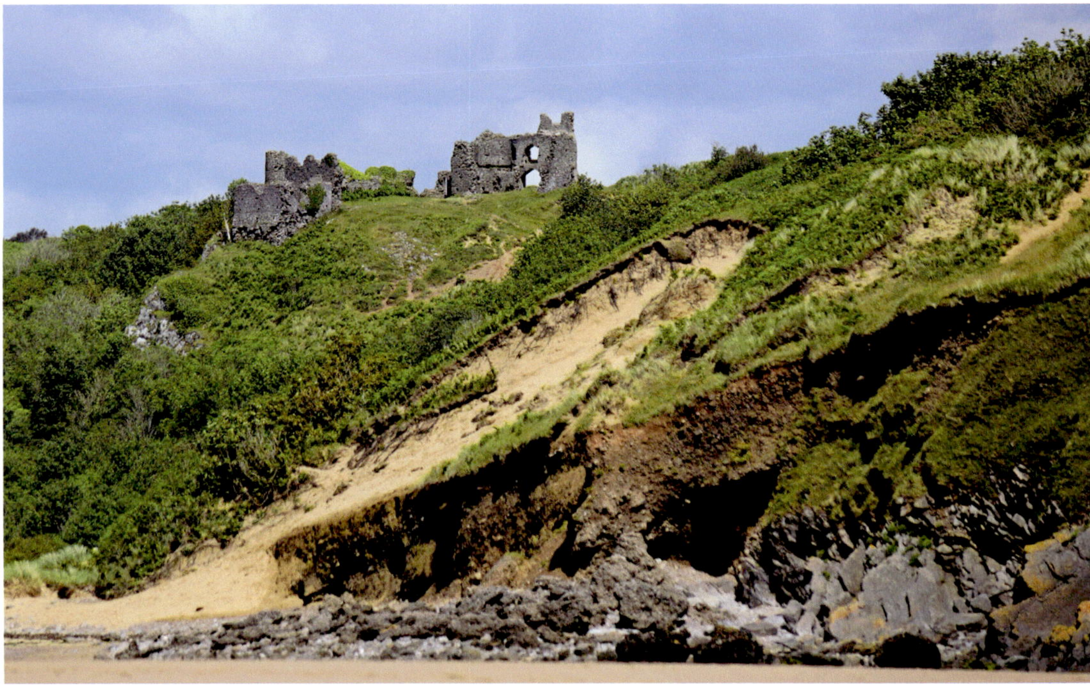

Pennard Castle. (© Mark Wordy, Flickr, CC BY 2.0)

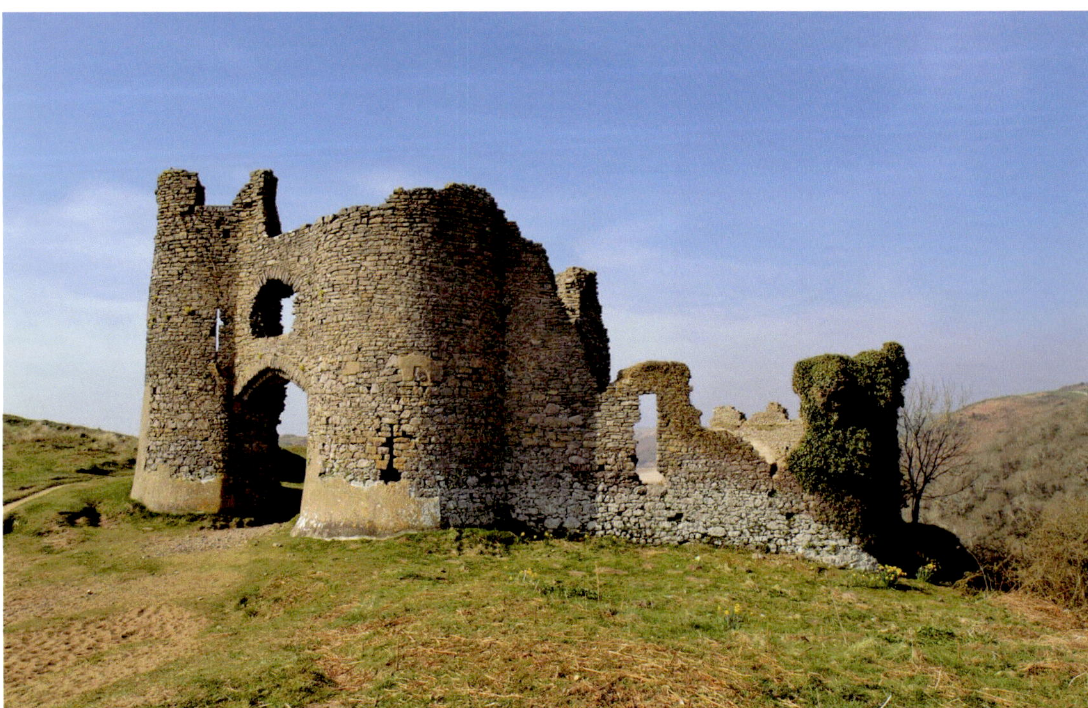

Pennard Castle. (© Gareth Lovering Photography, Flickr, CC BY-SA 2.0)

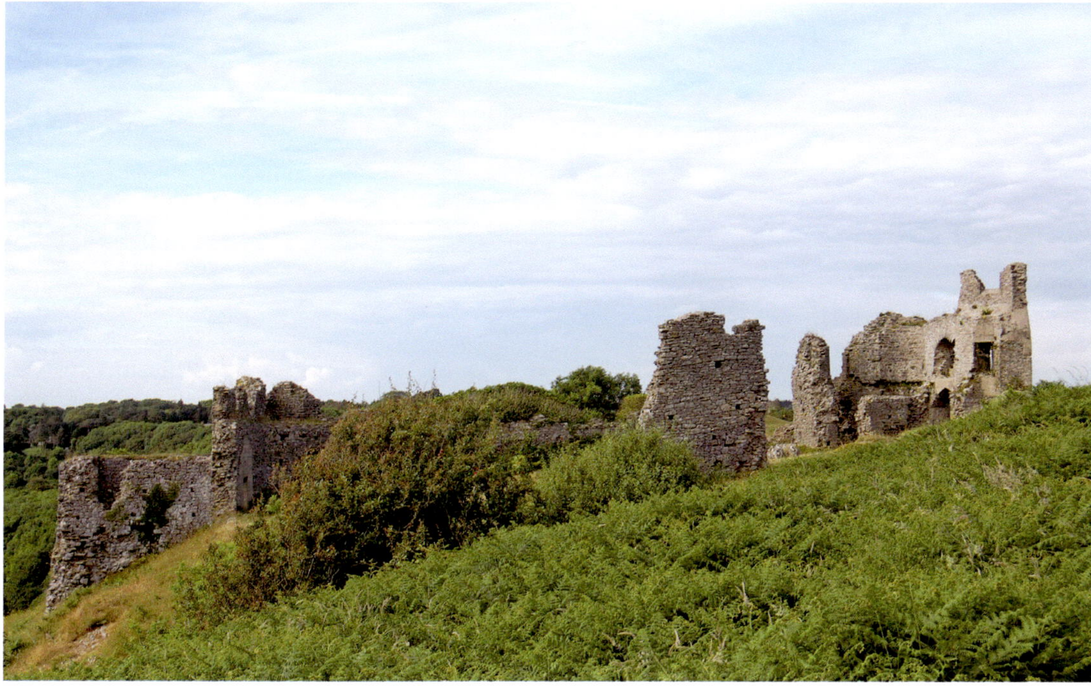

Pennard Castle. (© Simon Gibson, Flickr, CC BY-ND 2.0)

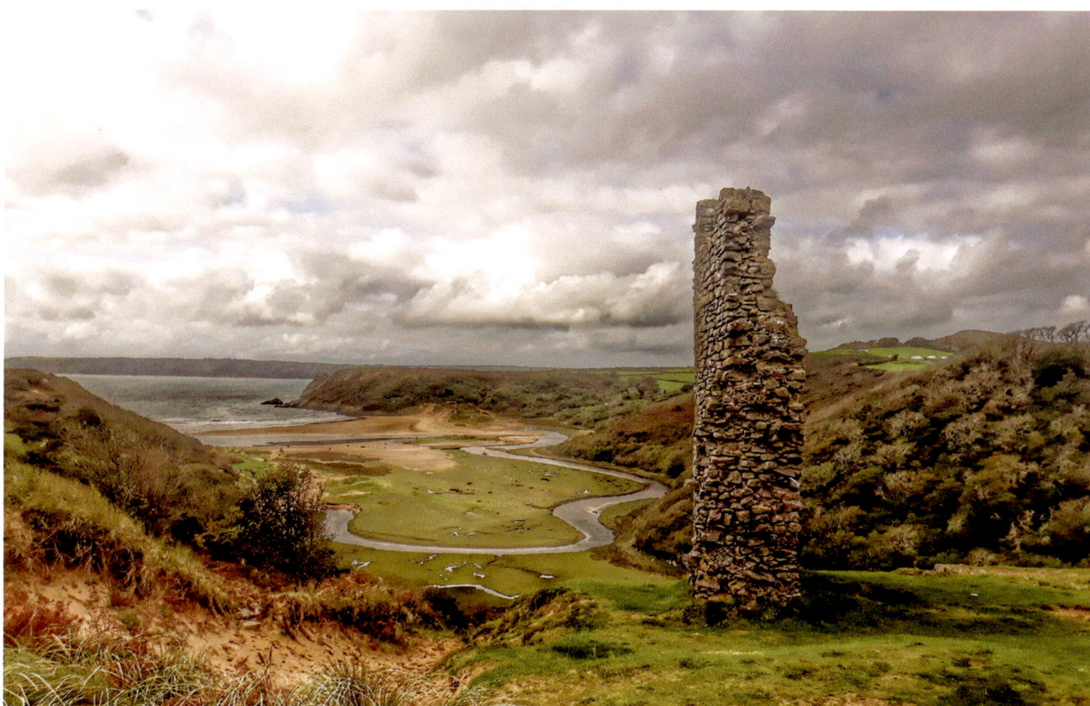

View of Three Cliffs Bay from Pennard Castle. (© Hefin Owen, Flickr, CC BY-SA 2.0)

me on the shoulder and whispered "something is playing games with us" and nodded in the direction of a section of ruined wall. Out of the corner of my eye I could see a shadowy form peeking at us, but as I turned my head to look, it seemed to duck out of sight, only to reappear when I looked away. I also saw a figure of a woman in big skirts, seemingly bending down and picking stuff up off the floor. This was a weird thing really, because it was just a very "eroded" shadow in the fog, but I got the clearest impression that's what it was. It only lasted a few seconds before swirling away in the breeze.' But that would not be his only encounter with the figure, who appeared a second time walking through the archway of the gatehouse: 'Originally, I figured it was a gap in the fog, because it moved in the direction of the wind, but then it moved *the other way*. It did this a few times, giving the impression of a guard patrolling the gate. The fog got thicker and we decided to call it a night.' As he walked through the spot where the figure had been he felt a sudden chill, and despite being very familiar with the area, discovered that the fog was so thick they were lost. This eventful Halloween has not, however, deterred Gregg from returning, and he says that despite his many visits, he has not seen anything since.

Flight of the Swan-maiden

Tales of so-called swan-maidens – women who can transform into swans – can be found across Europe, from Germanic legend to Irish folklore. Welsh swan-maidens are said to share many similarities with those of other countries, with one notable difference: they associate with *y tylwyth teg*, the Welsh fairy folk. In one tale from the Gower coast, a young farmer was busy working in a field when he saw a beautiful swan descend into the rocks. Creeping up for a closer look, he watched in amazement as it discarded its wings and feathers and transformed into 'a lovely maiden'. She bathed in the salty water, before changing back into bird form and flying away. From that day forth the farmer was obsessed and kept an eye out for his magical visitor, regularly spying on her as she took a sea bath. One day he decided to do more than watch and stole her garments, and when the distraught woman begged him to return her wings, he explained that he loved her too much to allow her to fly away. Her only option was to marry him, and with seemingly no alternative, she reluctantly agreed. For three years she played the part of the dutiful wife, until one day an opportunity presented itself. Her captor kept her wings under lock and key in an old oaken chest, and in a moment of carelessness he turned his back with the trunk wide open. She wasted no time in pouncing on her belongings and making a quick escape, and as she flew away, bid her husband farewell from on high. The inconsolable farmer was heartbroken and died within months, but the swan-maiden was free to spread her wings once more.

Arthur's Stone

Arthur's Stone (Maen Ceti) in Reynoldston has been described as Gower's most famous grave. Standing on the highest ridge of Cefn Bryn, it consists of a giant capstone perched on top of a group of smaller stones. There has long been talk of the area being haunted, and even Dylan Thomas, so the story goes, once took a group of amateur actors there to invoke the spirits. It is assumed the stones were brought to Cefn Bryn to form part of a double-chambered Neolithic tomb, and the capstone is exceptionally large, even by capstone standards. It was once even larger, with a sizable chunk of rock now lying next to it on the grass which, according to Iolo Morganwg, was hacked off by St David to stop the druids from worshipping false gods. He would presumably not be best pleased to hear that today it is a popular place of pagan pilgrimage. There was also a rather fanciful rumour that it was used for human sacrifice, based solely on the fact that perfectly natural red specs can be seen in the rock, that it was claimed represented blood. Other theories as to why the capstone was cut in two include being struck by lightning, a greedy miller who carved it off but found it too heavy to move, and the most likely, that a hairline crack appeared due to its exposed position to the elements.

Arthur's Stone, as its English-language name suggests, has a connection with the legendary king of Britain. As Arthur was walking along the Carmarthenshire coast, or the Neath Valley in an alternative version of the story, deep in thought ahead of the Battle of Camlann, he found it difficult to concentrate. A small stone in his shoe was disturbing him, so he stopped, removed it, and hurled it across the Loughor Estuary. It landed in its current location where it swelled in size having been touched by such an illustrious hand. While this tale is clearly a legend, there have been sightings of a spectral knight in the area that has led some to link the two together. Folklore also speaks of how the stone can move by itself and heads to the water for a drink before dawn. It is also a place for finding romance, and young maidens who want to check the fidelity of their sweethearts should follow a very specific set of instructions. At midnight during a full moon, place a cake of barley-meal and honey, which has been wetted with milk and well kneaded, on the stone as an offering. Then crawl around it three times on your hands and knees which, considering the rough and rugged terrain, gives new meaning to the expression 'love hurts'. Finally, if a ghostly vision of your lover materialises, it is a sign of their devotion. If they do not, they are potential heartbreakers.

Just a short drive from Arthur's Stone is another collection of stones that are also supposedly haunted by 'something'. The Parc Cwm long cairn in Green Cwm, a Neolithic burial chamber sheltered by ancient trees, has an uncanny atmosphere where visitors feel compelled to lower their voices in respect for some ancient presence. People have reported finding the eerie silence unnerving, and the feeling of being watched as if someone – or something – is there with them.

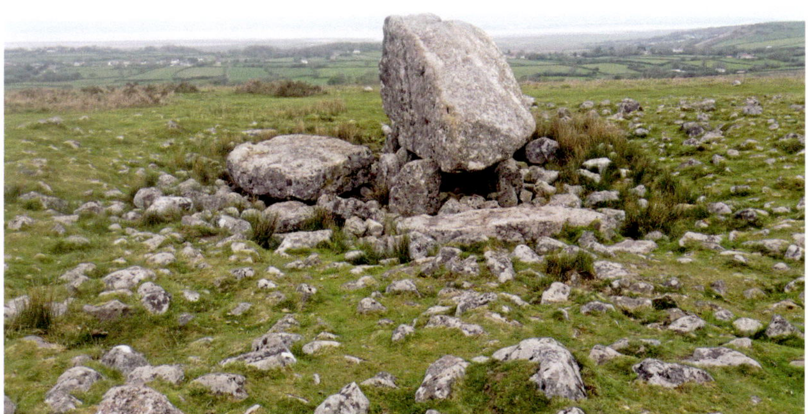

Arthur's Stone (Maen Ceti).

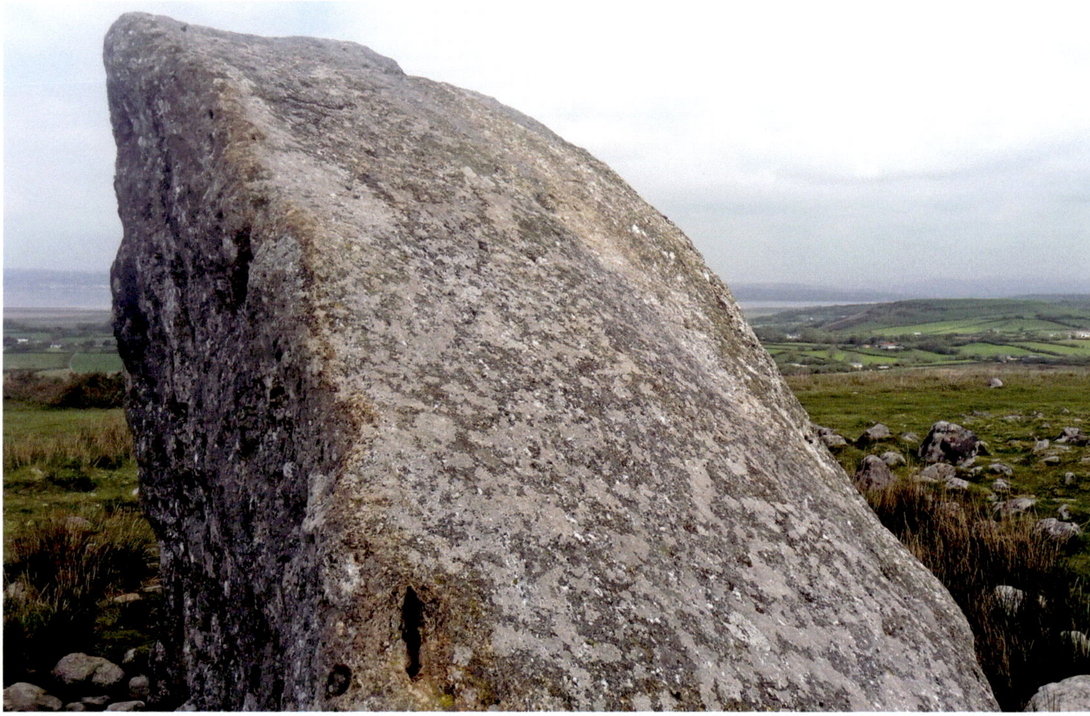

Arthur's Stone's capstone.

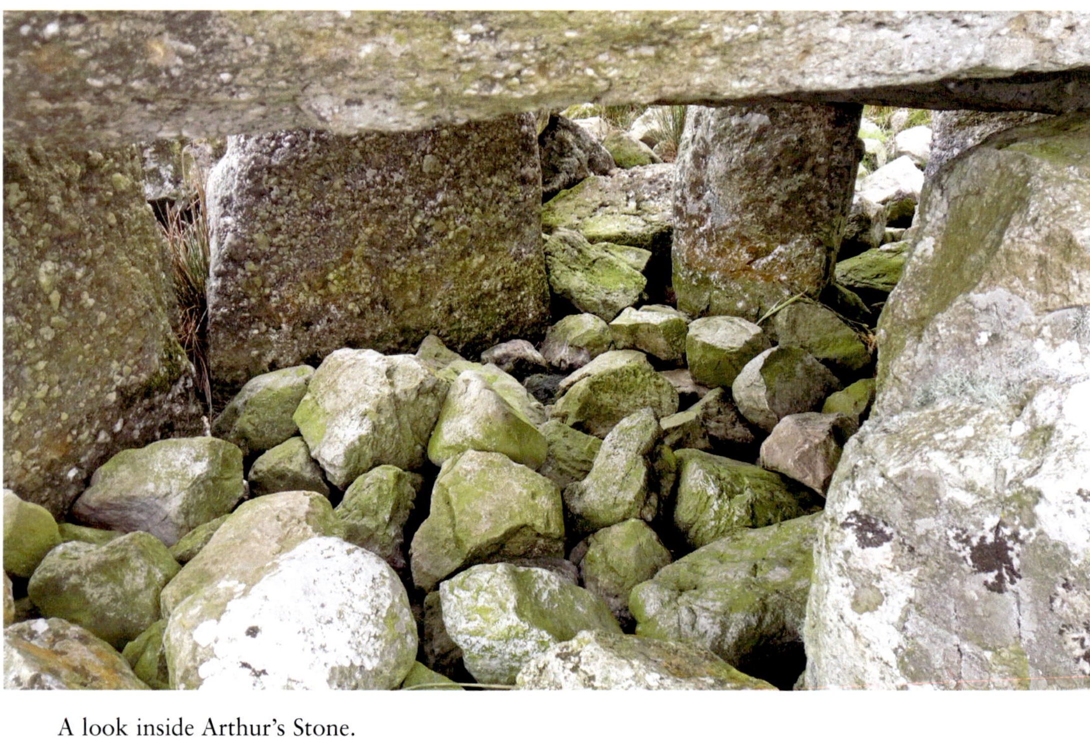

A look inside Arthur's Stone.

Haunted History

The most historical areas of Swansea and Gower are also, unsurprisingly, said to be the most haunted. These ancient bays and mighty fortresses have borne witness to much murder and mayhem over the centuries, and as a result, many souls have lost their lives sooner than they would have wished. While some of the folkloric tales in the opening chapter might be difficult for the modern reader to accept, as we progress through time the accounts become increasingly credible, and they all suggest the same thing: from mighty battles to medieval conspiracies, many of those who died too soon do not rest easy.

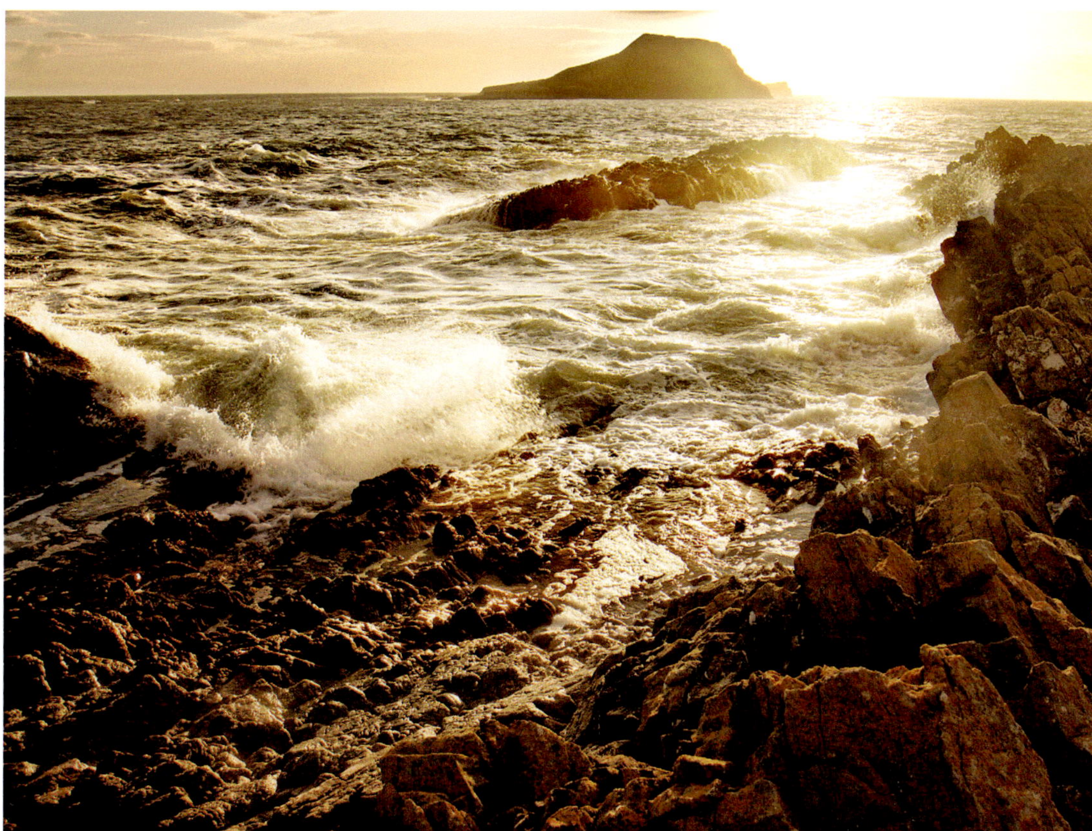

The waves crash on Rhossili Bay. (© Michael Warren, Flickr, CC BY 2.0)

Rhossili Bay

Rhossili Old Rectory stands in an idyllic, if somewhat lonely, spot overlooking Rhossili's sprawling bay. From this vantage point, Worm's Head can be seen jutting out to sea, a striking headland that derives its name from the Old English word *wyrm,* meaning sea serpent or dragon, because of its resemblance to one of these mythological creatures. Now renovated and cared for by the National Trust, the Grade II listed house dates from the mid-nineteenth century, while much older farmyard buildings can be found dotted outside. Its secluded location was originally chosen for practical reasons, having been built for the Revd John Lloyd who served both Rhossili and neighbouring Llangennith and needed somewhere between the two. When it was later decided to relocate the rectory closer to the church in Rhossili the house became known as the 'old' rectory, and this is when reports of a haunting began to emerge. Occupants claim to have felt sudden icy chills, heard a disembodied voice whispering in their ear, and members of the clergy have even reported seeing full-bodied apparitions. It has been suggested that the source of the disturbances might emerge from the sea on dark winter nights and make their way up the path to disturb those living on land.

The paranormal activity is not limited to the rectory. The sand itself is said to be haunted by the ghost of Revd John Ponsonby Lucas, the rectory's longest-serving vicar before relocation, who still rides his black stallion at night. The waves have claimed many a ship over the years such as the *Helvetia*, a Norwegian oak barque that was wrecked on Halloween in 1887, its rotting timbers now protruding from the sand as a permanent reminder of the tragedy. A ghost story that relates to another shipwreck tells of how the *Dollar Ship* crashed ashore in the seventeenth century with a hoard of Spanish bullion. The lord and lady of Rhossili quickly readied their carriage and set off to claim the loot, brushing aside anyone else with the same idea, but they did not have long to enjoy their ill-gotten gains and were murdered soon after. They are now doomed to relive that fateful night, and whenever a storm arises a coach drawn by headless horses might be seen charging along the sand. In an alternative version of the tale, it was a member of the Mansel family who stole the gold, before escaping to Ireland where they blew it on drink.

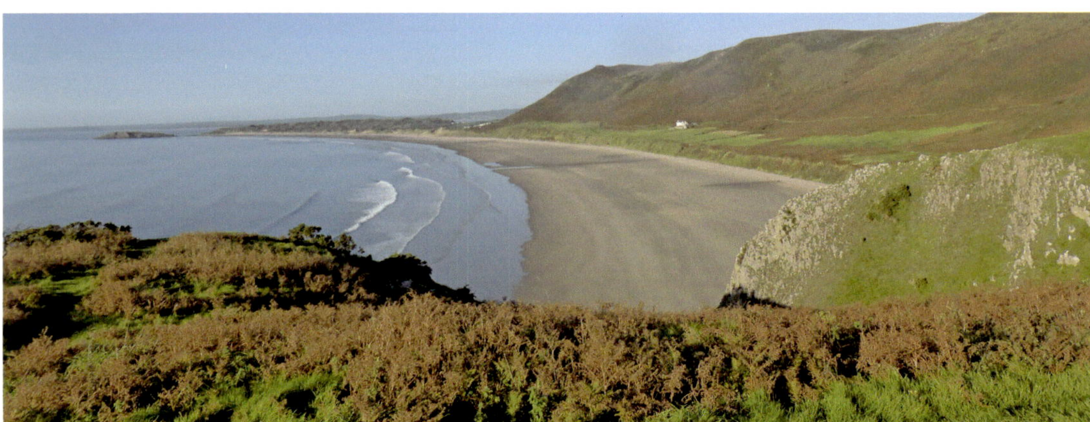

Rhossili Bay. (© Andrew Bone, Flickr, CC BY 2.0)

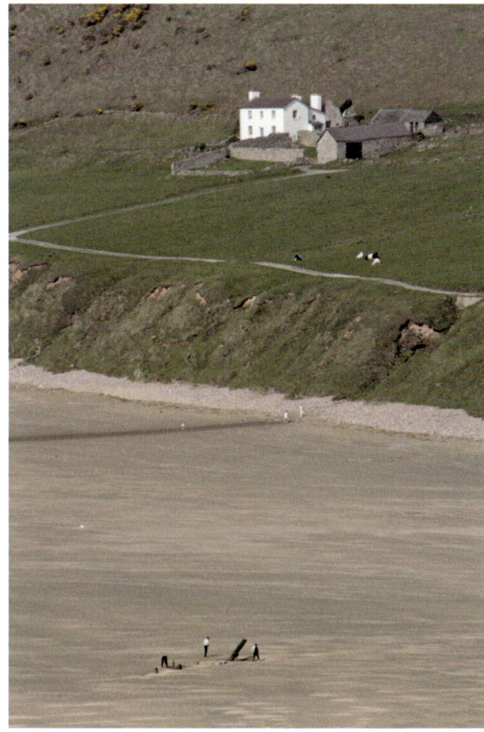

Rhossili Old Rectory from the southern cliffs.
(© Jo and Steve Turner, CC BY-SA 2.0)

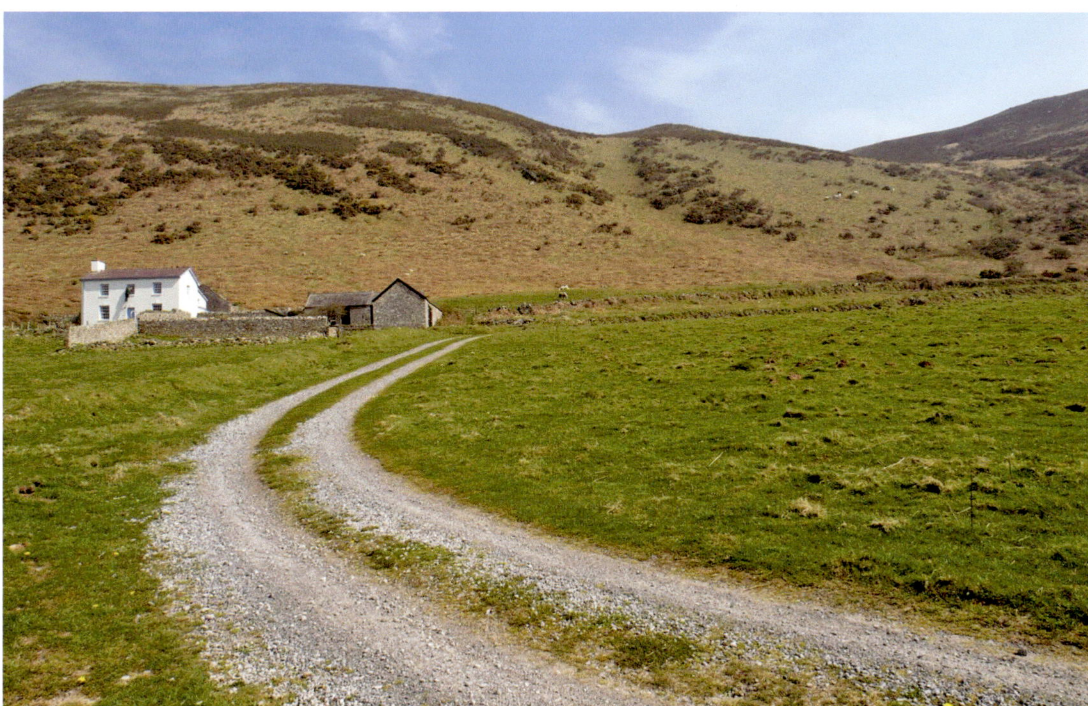

Rhossili Old Rectory. (© Gareth Lovering, Flickr, CC BY-SA 2.0)

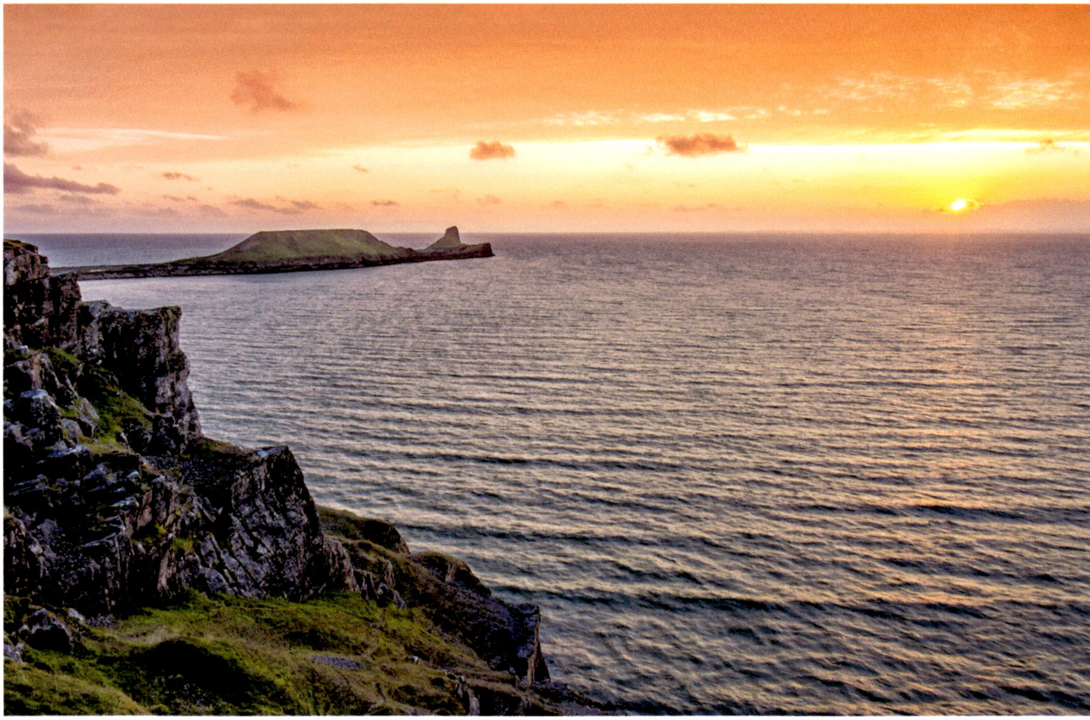

Worm's Head, Rhossili Bay. (© Stewart Black, Flickr, CC BY 2.0)

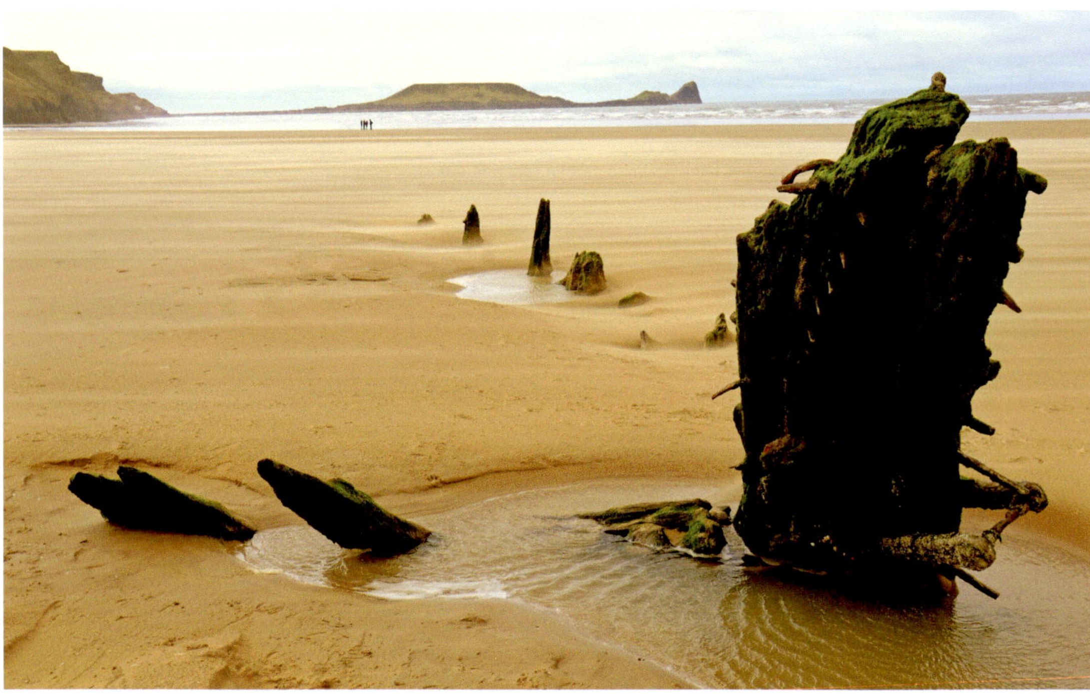

Shipwreck on Rhossili Bay. (© Richard Whitaker, Flickr, CC BY 2.0)

Oystermouth Castle

Oystermouth Castle is home to arguably Swansea's most famous ghost: the White Lady. This spectral woman watches over Mumbles by night from the battlements and can be encountered both inside and outside the Norman fortress. While her identity remains a mystery, one suggestion is that she could be the spirit of Alina de Mowbray, the eldest daughter of William de Braose, Lord of Gower. The castle became the family home in the thirteenth century, and among their many upgrades was the addition of a personal chapel. Having been restored and reopened to the public in 2011, it is now named Alina's Chapel in honour of the family member believed to have been the driving force behind its creation.

A legend published in 1879 suggests a different identity. It tells of a time when the castle was in the care of Earl Neville, a vicious Norman lord who imprisoned a monk following a perceived slight and abandoned him to starve in the dungeon. A deeply pious guard working at the castle did what little he could to keep the monk alive by concealing morsels of food in a pillar in his cell. It only served to delay the inevitable, but before the monk died, he said to his kind protector: 'If any good man or woman, free of sin, should come to the pillar, and pray there, and pace around it nine times, his or her wish would be granted.' Soon afterwards, during a raid in Ireland, the earl once again shocked his devout companions by ignoring the rules of combat and burning down a bishop's palace. Everyone was slaughtered except for one captive, the bishop's niece who he claimed as his wife. She was desperately unhappy back in Oystermouth Castle but was kind to those who worked there, who in return took pity on the nice 'white lady', a nickname that referred to the colour of her clothing. In a bid to save her from Neville she was told about the monk's final words and, with nothing to lose, she crept into the dungeon to the 'wishing post' while her husband was away hunting in Gower. She followed the instructions exactly, and the next morning her maid was surprised to discover that her wish had been granted, but not in a way that anyone had expected. The 'white lady' was at peace and finally free; she was dead.

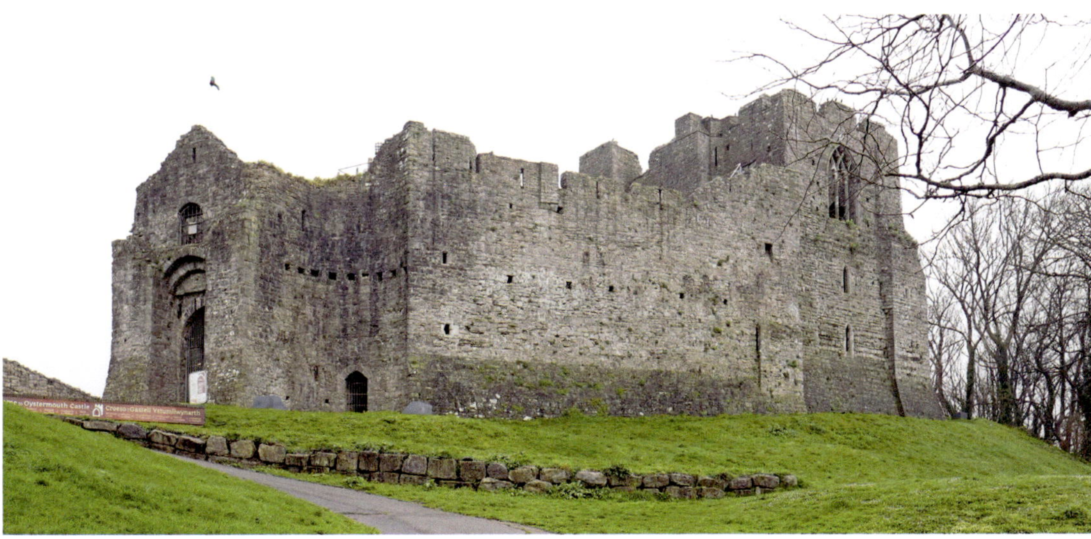

Oystermouth Castle. (© Malcolm Murdoch, Flickr, CC BY-SA 2.0)

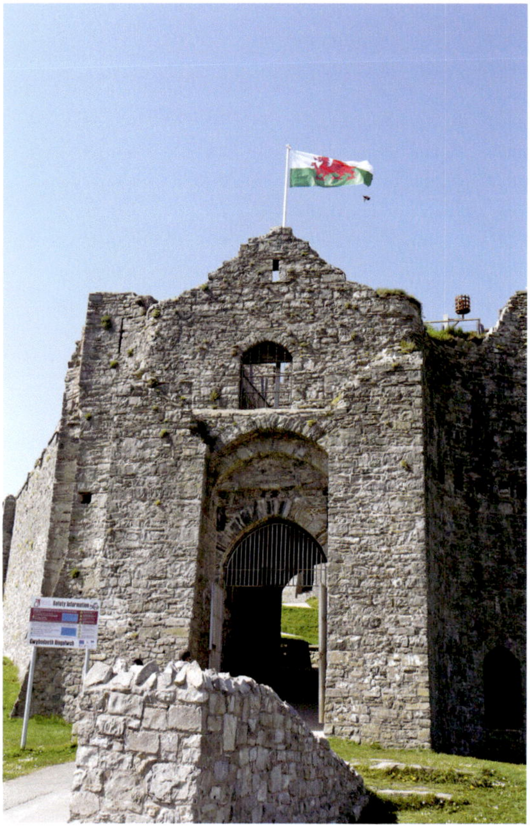

Entrance to Oystermouth Castle. (© Malcolm Murdoch, Flickr, CC BY-SA 2.0)

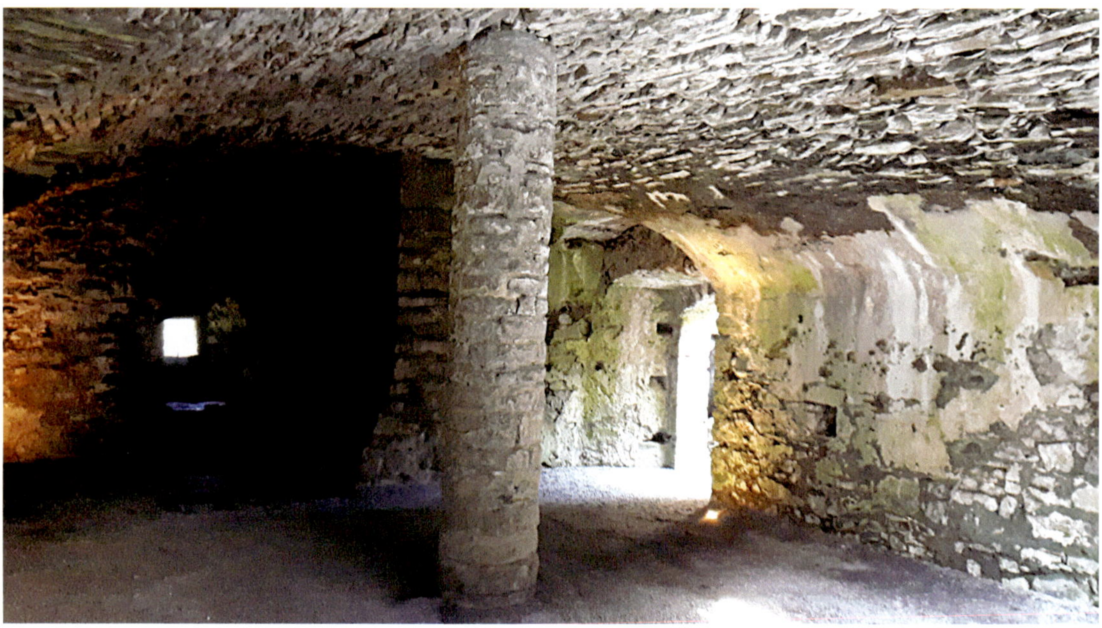

The post inside Oystermouth Castle.

An alternative version of the monk's instructions has long been used by youngsters in search of love or a fright. It is said that if you walk around the post nine times while sticking a pin in it and looking at the wall the white lady will appear. When ghost hunter Peter Underwood did just that in the 1970s she did not, sadly, appear for him, but he did speak to some locals who she did apparently appear for. Their accounts suggested that the post in the cell was not the 'wishing post' of legend but something far grislier: a 'whipping post'. One man recalled how, during a family picnic on the grounds, his two children pointed out a woman behind a tree who was crying but made no sound. As she turned to flee from his prying eyes, he saw her torn clothing and bloodied skin. On separate occasions, a young couple heard crying and noticed a similar-looking woman disappear behind a tree, while a dog walker's dog was frozen in fright after witnessing a ghost-like woman vanish through the castle's stone wall. In more recent times, just like Underwood, I have also been unsuccessful in my attempts to catch a glimpse of the White Lady despite following the instructions, but I can confirm that it's a wonderfully atmospheric castle to visit, ghosts or otherwise.

The Demon House

In the mid-seventeenth century, the British public were captivated by reports of 'supernatural disturbances' in a Gower home. It concerned the estate of army officer Henry Bowen in Llanelen, an area just east of Llanrhidian that gained a rather ominous nickname: 'the village of the dead'. Excavations have revealed that Llanelen was occupied from at least the sixth century, and the remains of a church and dozens of graves have been discovered there. Legend speaks of how the survivors of a shipwreck in the Burry Estuary were cared for by the good people of Llanelen, but

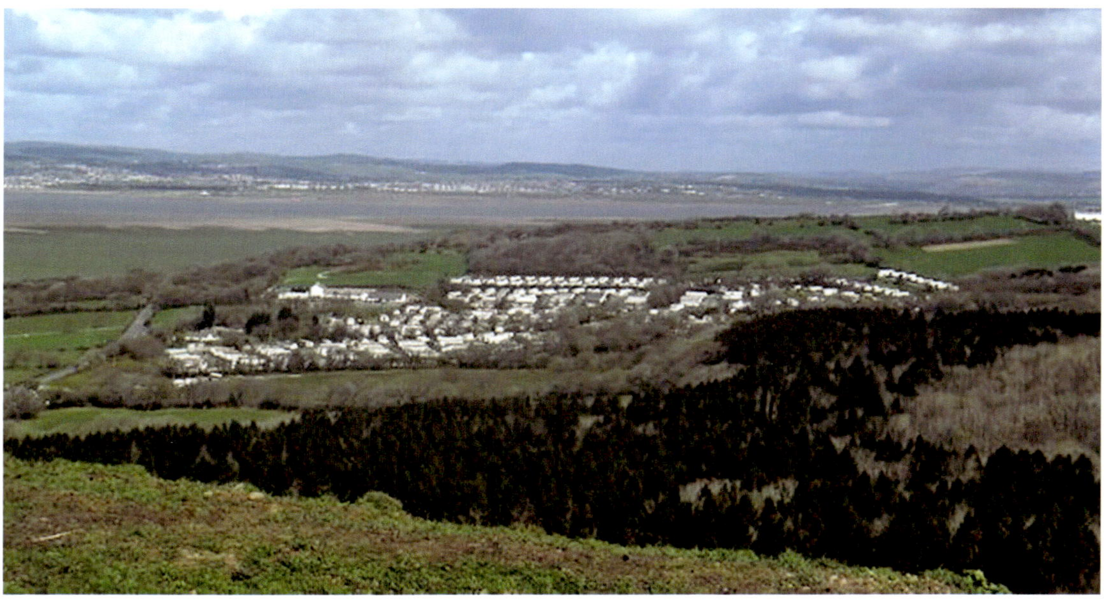

Overlooking the caravan park in Llanrhidian near the sight of Llanellen. (© Kevin Corcoran, CC BY-SA 2.0)

this act of Christian charity proved to be costly when it was discovered that they were carrying the plague. It spread like wildfire, and now the only villager who remains is a mysterious white lady who walks among the lonely stones that are unlucky to touch. A stone inscribed in memory of the village can be seen in the gate of Ss Rhydian and Illtyd.

The details of the demonic activity at Bowen's house were initially recorded in a series of letters written in 1656. Bowen is described as a fervent Christian who lost his faith after fighting in the Civil War and turned to drink after turning his back on God. He drank so heavily that he was sent away to Ireland on service while his wife remained at their home in Gower, and with her husband overseas the trouble began. There was banging at the doors and windows that shook the house so violently she thought it might fall over. One night as she was retiring to bed, she was startled to find a man standing next to her who looked just like her husband. He asked if he should join her between the bedsheets, and sensing that this was no mortal man she refused. He pleaded and protested but she insisted that Christ was her husband and prayed until he was repelled, a terrible wailing sound drifting through the house in his wake. The following night, prominent members of the local congregation joined Mrs Bowen in her prayers, and all was peaceful once more. On the next night, however, the activity returned with greater ferocity. Thick smoke that smelt of sulphur darkened her chamber, and as she entered her bed, she noticed what appeared to be the impression of a body on the covers next to her. It looked as if somebody had been lying there, and there was an unsufferable stench that was compared to a putrefied carcass. She suddenly realised she was not alone in the bed, and the invisible entity began to roll back and forth until she was pushed out. Mrs Bowen cried for help, her tormentor cried in delight, and her two maids rushed in and joined her in praying next to the bed. The uninvited bedfellow did its best to interrupt them, and at one point Mrs Bowen felt herself being lifted a foot or more from the ground by what felt like a dog under her knees. They continued in their fervent praying and the evil presence stormed up and down the stairs in a rage, cursing them and blowing the candles. When all else failed it began to physically strike them, but they continued in their devotions for some six hours, only to discover their bodies beaten and bruised the next day. While they might have repelled the 'demon' on this occasion, the attacks became a regular occurrence and Mrs Bowen was forced to accept defeat and fled to stay with her mother. She sent word to her husband who returned to Britain four months later, but his lifestyle had not improved and, despite his wife fearing for her life, he sent his family back to Gower while he returned to Cork. It was suggested that he was 'haunted' for the rest of his life, if not by evil spirits, then certainly by his selfish decisions. As one acquaintance wrote: 'if ever a blasphemer was unworthy to live, this is the Man'.

The Red Lady of Paviland

Goat's Hole (Paviland Cave) is a site of huge arachnological importance. A picturesque if hazardous limestone cave between Port Eynon and Rhossili, it is also said to be haunted, and a groundbreaking discovery made there in the nineteenth century might offer a clue as to who, or what, calls it home. It was during a dig in 1823 that William Buckland, Professor of Geology at Oxford University, discovered half a skeleton just inside the entrance. Human skeletons weren't really his speciality, but he assumed it was a female from the Roman period and, as it was stained with red ochre, 'she' became known as the Red Lady of Paviland. It was further speculated that she had been a prostitute or a witch based purely on the fact that they were two female occupations that required a certain level of secrecy. Reports of a ghostly woman haunting the cave soon emerged, with some describing her as a wizened old witch who cackled from behind the rocks. This certainly matched one of the theories, until a quite sizeable problem emerged: the skeleton was neither female nor Roman. The male was more accurately dated to the Upper Palaeolithic period and the skeleton became known as the 'oldest known ceremonial burial in Western Europe'. This did nothing to dampen the reports of a haunting, merely that the resident ghost and the skeleton might not be one and the same, with another theory suggesting it was a treasure hunter who had been caught out by the treacherous tide.

The Red Lady isn't the only skeleton to be found in a supposedly haunted and out-of-the-way location in Gower. In the 1920s, as a couple walked up the footpath from Brandy Cove, they heard the screams of a woman and turned back to investigate. They traced the sound to the caves, but when the screaming stopped and with night falling, they were forced to give up the search. A few days later a fisherman from Murton heard a similar sound, and as the reports continued, people began to speculate that maybe a woman who had gone missing a few years earlier might be making her location known. In 1961, a female skeleton was discovered in the area, and she was given a proper burial in Bishopston.

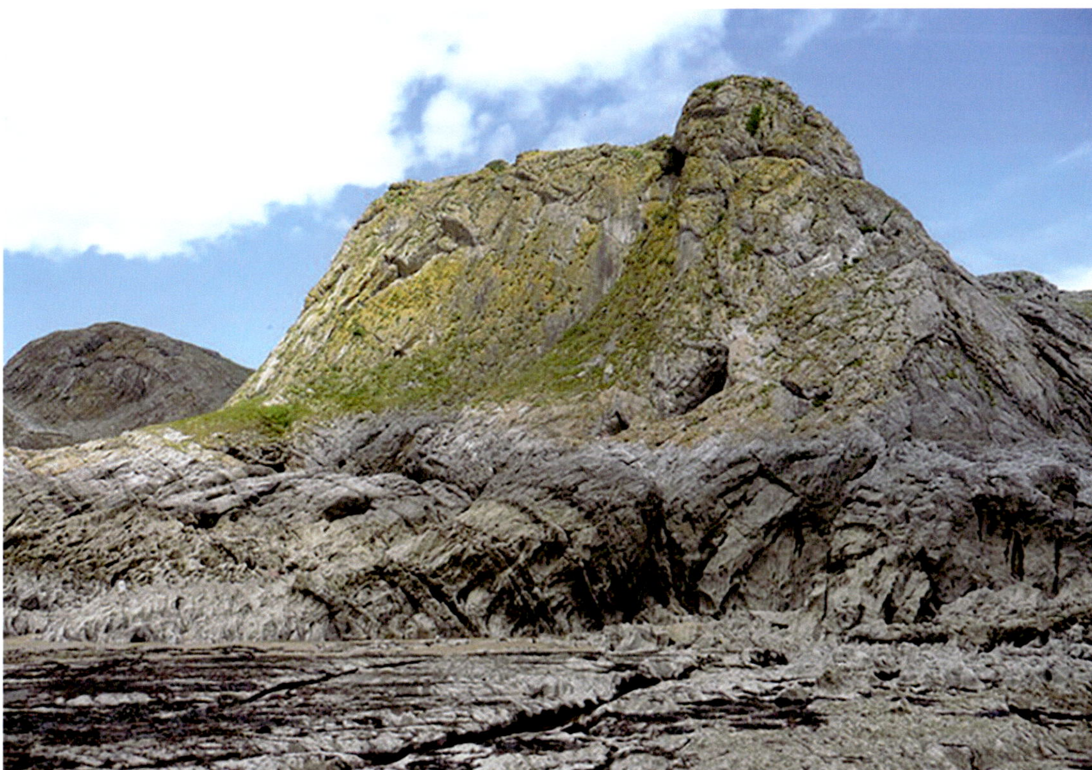

Paviland Cave. (© Jeremy Bolwell, CC BY-SA 2.0)

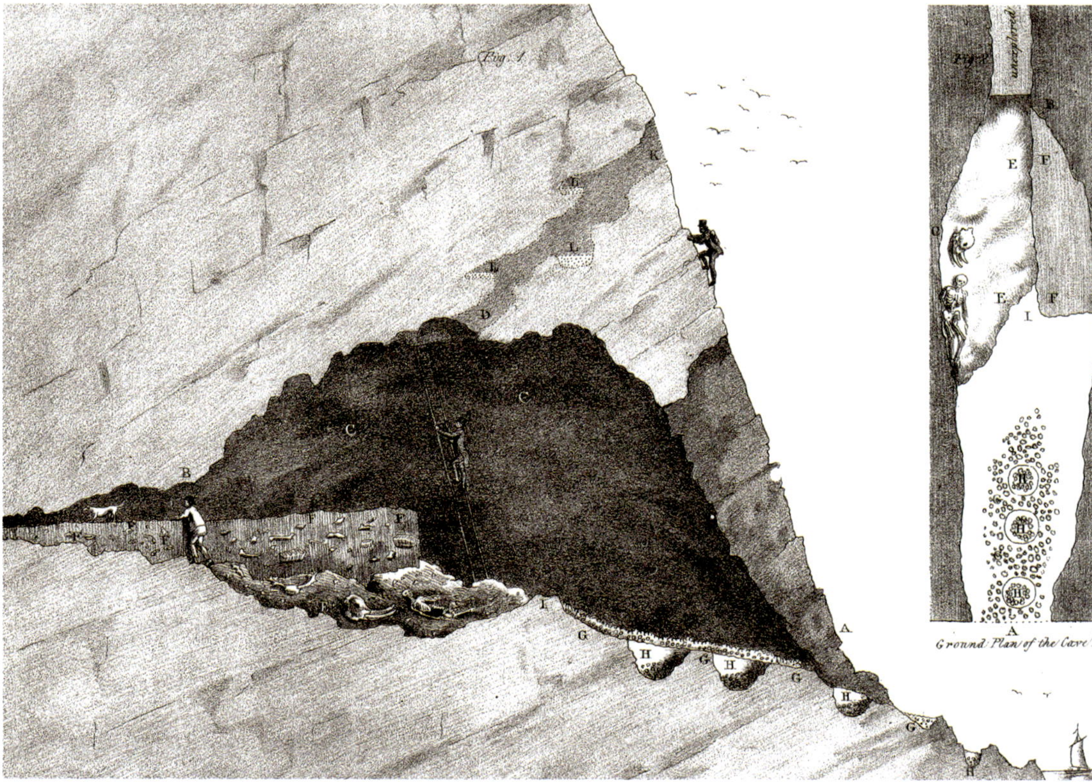

Section of Paviland Cave. (© Wellcome Images, CC BY 4.0)

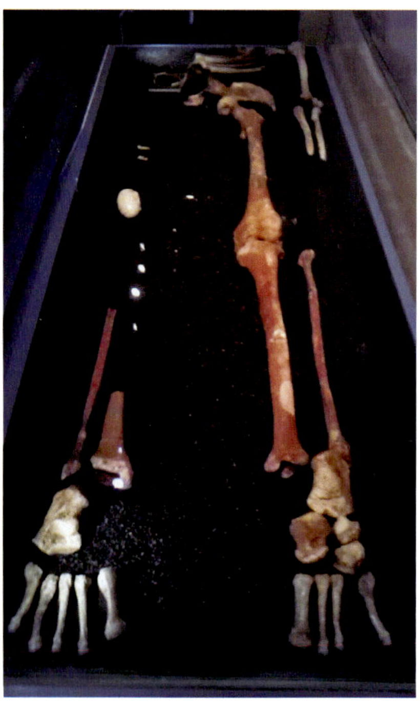

Red Lady of Paviland on display. (© Ethan Doyle White, CC BY-SA 3.0)

Port Eynon Salt House

The Salt House overlooking Port Eynon Point is home to a romantic legend that might offer some clues as to the paranormal activity reported within. Now a set of atmospheric ruins, the scheduled monument is believed to have been built in the sixteenth century as a saltworks that was later fortified to protect its valuable produce. According to the story, it also became the headquarters of John Lucas, a notorious pirate and smuggler who fortified it for more illicit reasons. He also created a secret underground passage that connected the Salt House with Culver Hole on the shore. This mysterious cave is sealed off behind a stone wall and difficult to access, making it ideal for covertly transporting goods from the sea to land. After Lucas died the family smuggling business continued until the 'great storm' of 1703, a natural disaster that caused unprecedented destruction across southern England and Wales. The Church of England declared it an act of vengeance from God, and that certainly appeared to be the case for the Salt House that was struck by lightning.

While this story combines elements of fact and fiction, the 'great storm' did permanently damage the Salt House, and the buildings standing today are the remains of cottages last occupied in the nineteenth century by oystermen. They are said to be home to several ghosts, possibly the spirits of Lucas and his rogues if the legend is to be believed. Spectral smugglers have also been reported on the bay below, where the sound of two warring families rings out in the night sky. Said to be the Mansel family, who Lucas closely associated with, clashing with the Herbert family, their rivalry can be heard from Oxwich Bay in the west to Rhossili Bay in the east.

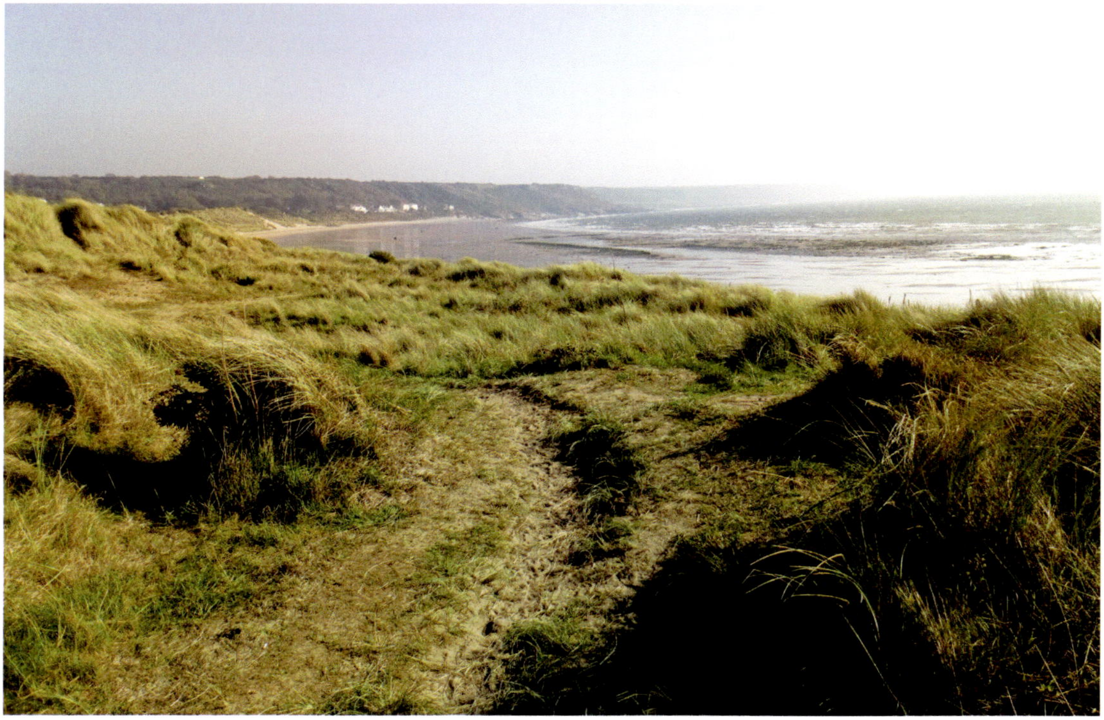

Port Eynon Bay. (© proby458 (Paul), Flickr, CC BY 2.0)

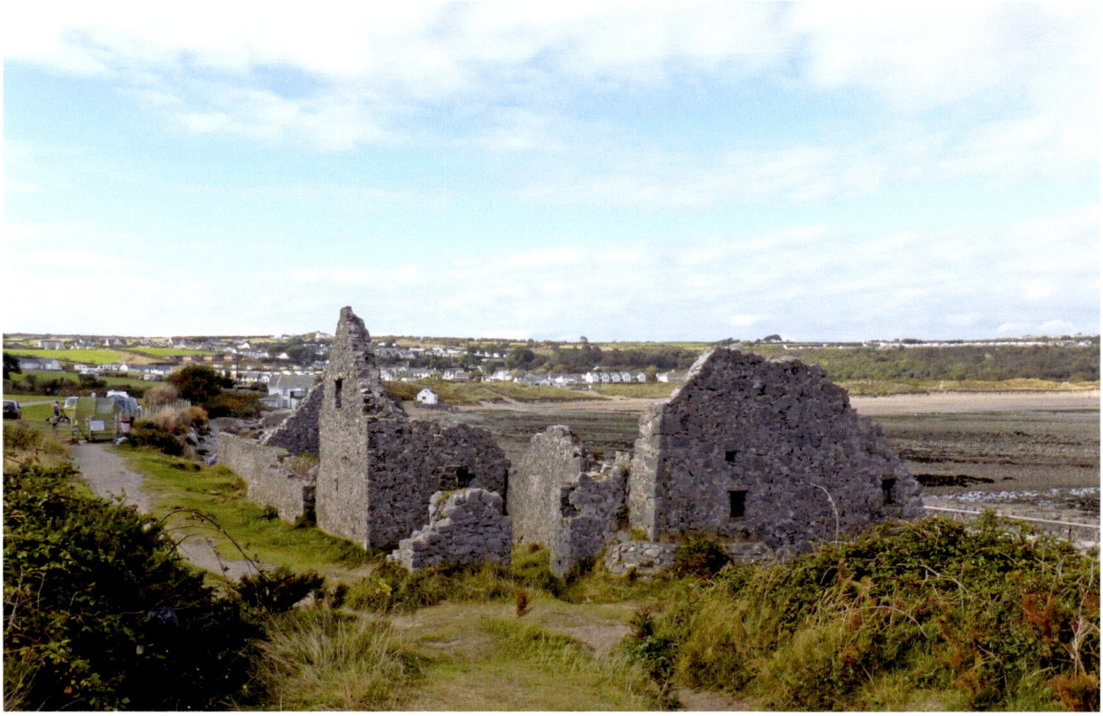

Port Eynon Salt House. (© Claire Cox, Flickr, CC BY-ND 2.0)

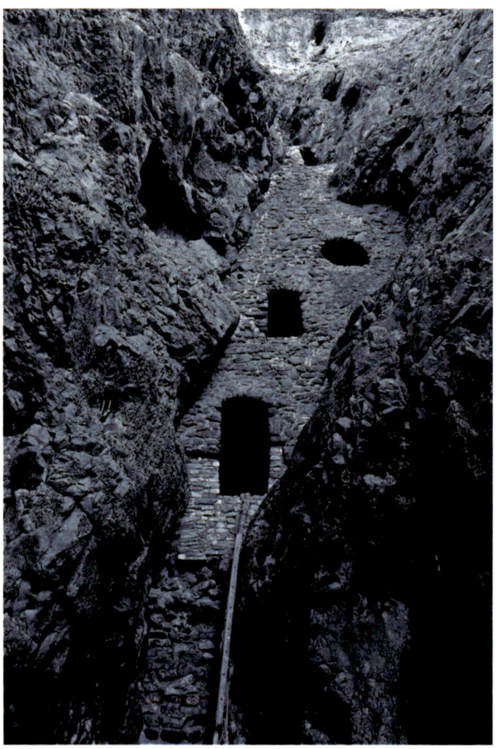

Culver Hole, Port Eynon. (© Andrew Bennett, Flickr, CC BY 2.0)

Whiteford Sands

Whiteford Point Lighthouse cuts a striking figure in the Burry Estuary. Now out of commission, the 44-foot-high cast-iron lighthouse off the coast of Whiteford Sands is a Grade II* listed building that dates from 1865. It warned many a sailor of the dangers of the submerged rocks and sandbank, and witnessed its fair share of shipwrecks, such as the Whiteford disaster of 1868 in which some sixteen ships and at least nineteen lives were lost in the bay. The fleet had set sail from Llanelli but were caught out by the changing conditions, and despite dropping anchor were pulled along the seabed, smashing into the rocks and each other. At what is assumed to be the same time the Revd John D. Davies of Cheriton and Llanmadoc heard a terrifying scream in the churchyard and rushed outside. He recalled that: 'I saw a young lad standing there, his face distorted with fright. He said he had seen a man without his hat come and look in through the window. The boy, being taken into the church, was some time in coming to himself. It was believed that what he saw was the ghost of one of the drowned men, as this was the very hour of the wrecks.' Some of the recovered bodies were buried in that church afterwards.

Nowadays, it is unwary beachgoers who need to be warned of the ever-changing tide and the hundreds – yes, hundreds – of ghosts said to haunt the 2-mile stretch of bay. As with Port Eynon, this vast collection of spirits is believed to be two opposing armies locked in an endless war, with the sounds of charging feet echoing around the beauty spot. The noises begin as a murmur in Broughton Bay and grow to a deafening crescendo on Whiteford Sands where the main duel is assumed to take

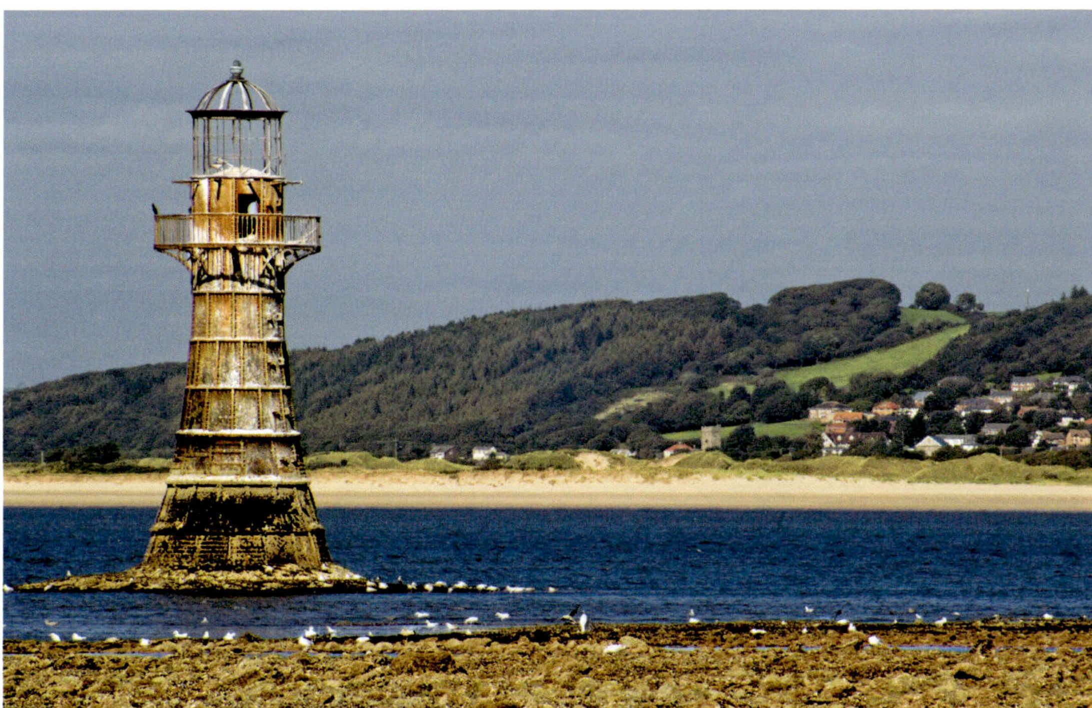

Whiteford Point Lighthouse. (© S P L, Flickr, CC BY-SA 2.0)

place. Who exactly is fighting is open to debate, but a popular suggestion based on historical encounters is that an army of Celtic warriors are attempting to repel the Roman invaders, or possibly a clash between Viking and Norman forces. Another theory goes even further back in time to the Ice Age, arguing that because the footsteps are so loud, they couldn't possibly be caused by humans, even on horseback, leading to speculation that ghostly woolly mammoths might be to blame. As bizarre as that may sound, in the nineteenth century a group of cockle-picking women heard a galloping sound and turned to see what they described as a giant woolly animal with a horn above the snout that stampeded down the sand. It caused chaos among the carts and they gave north Gower a wide berth as a result. A similar creature was also spotted in the salt marshes of Llanrhidian that, according to the tale, was banished by a local witch. At dusk, she walked through the trees of Whiteford Burroughs towards the water's edge and drew a magic circle, inside of which she placed Dead Man's Fingers, a seaweed used for laverbread. This summoned the beast and, as it charged towards her, she shouted some magical words that trapped it in the circle where it became mist and vanished.

A far nastier tale from the nineteenth century speaks of a cruel farmer from Llanmadoc who married a local girl and treated her appallingly. One night, following a heavy session in the pub, he returned home and beat her until she fled for her life onto Whiteford Burrows. He gave chase but it was too dark, and he was too drunk, to find her, so he returned the next morning on his grey stallion and spotted her heading towards Broughton Bay. He chased her down with such ferocity that she was swept under the horse's feet, and not content with simply wounding her he turned the horse around and trampled over her repeatedly until she was dead. His spirit, it is said, along with the horse, return to haunt the sands today. As a final footnote to these accounts of eerie sounds on the sand, the spirits of youngsters dressed in 1950s rock and roll gear partying late into the night have also been reported. Could they be the real reason there's a whole lot of shakin' going on?

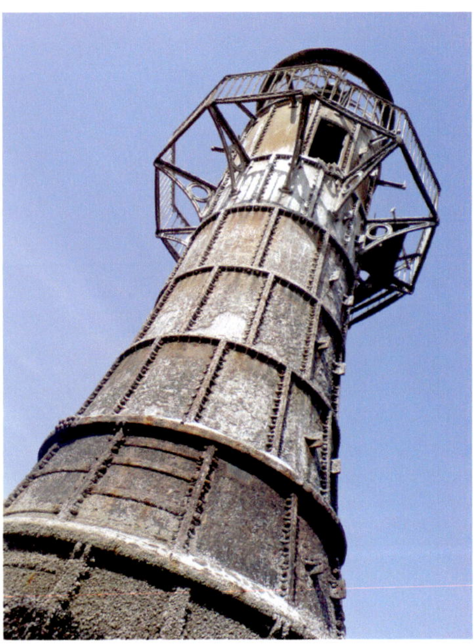

Whiteford Point Lighthouse. (© Thomas Guest, Flickr, CC BY 2.0)

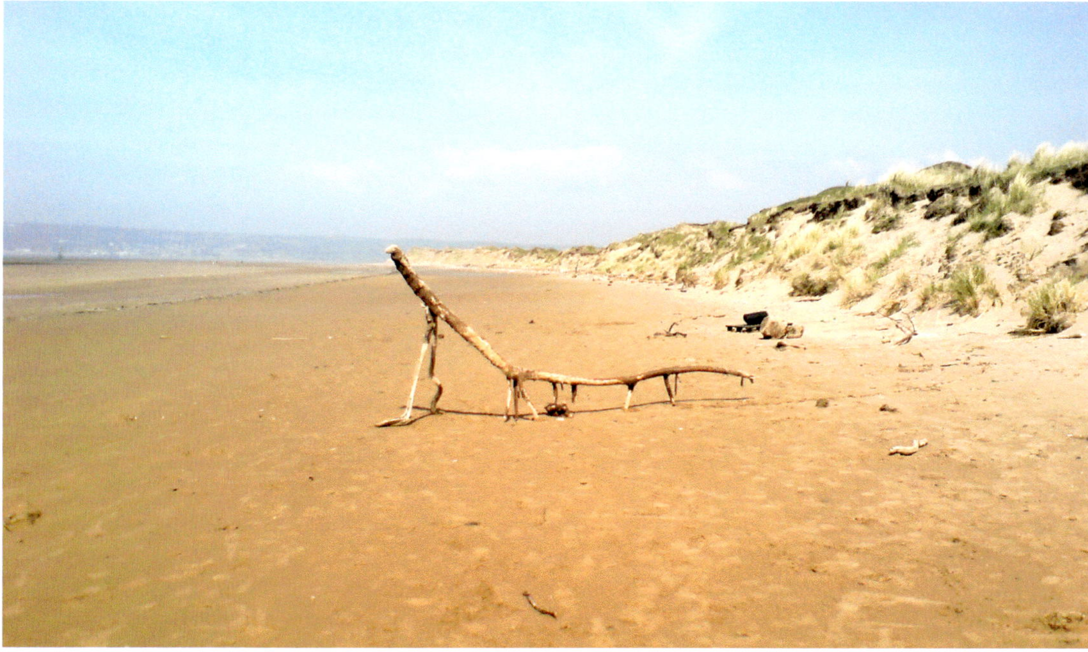

Flotsam and jetsam on Whiteford Sands. (© Thomas Guest, Flickr, CC BY 2.0)

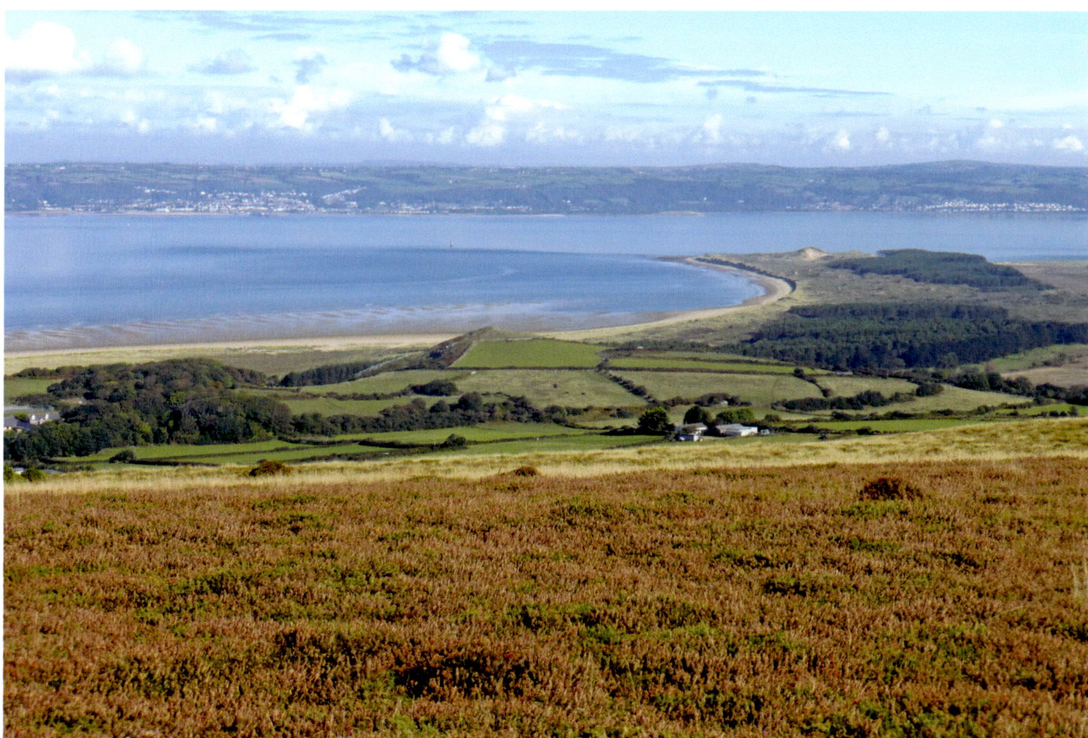

Whiteford Sands looking across to Burry Port. (© Claire Cox, Flickr, CC BY-ND 2.0)

Mumbles Lighthouse

While its days as a life-saving beacon are a thing of the past, Mumbles Lighthouse now serves a more aesthetic role as one of the most photogenic landmarks in a village blessed with photogenic landmarks. Built off Mumbles Head in 1794, a legend associated with the island tells of an elderly monk who set up home in one of its caves many centuries ago. He established a secret cell among the rocks where he could be left alone to his private contemplations and spent hours each day spying on the boats as they sailed the waves. One day, a ship came closer than expected, and when he realised they were landing, he went to greet them. Three men came ashore with solemn expressions on their faces carrying the cause of their sadness: the dead body of a young man with a handsome face. They were looking to dispose of the corpse on the rocks, and when they saw the holy man asked if he would pray for the departed's soul. This he was happy to do, and so they placed the body inside his cave and left some money for his services – not that he had any use for it. He also suspected that foul play might have been involved in the man's death, and they might have paid him with loot stolen from the victim. The men set off to sea once more and the man of God prayed long and hard for the deceased's salvation but, it would appear, he was unsuccessful. His tormented soul does not rest easy and is heard wailing in pain to this day. It is said that he will continue to do so until his body is given a suitable burial in consecrated ground – a seemingly impossible request.

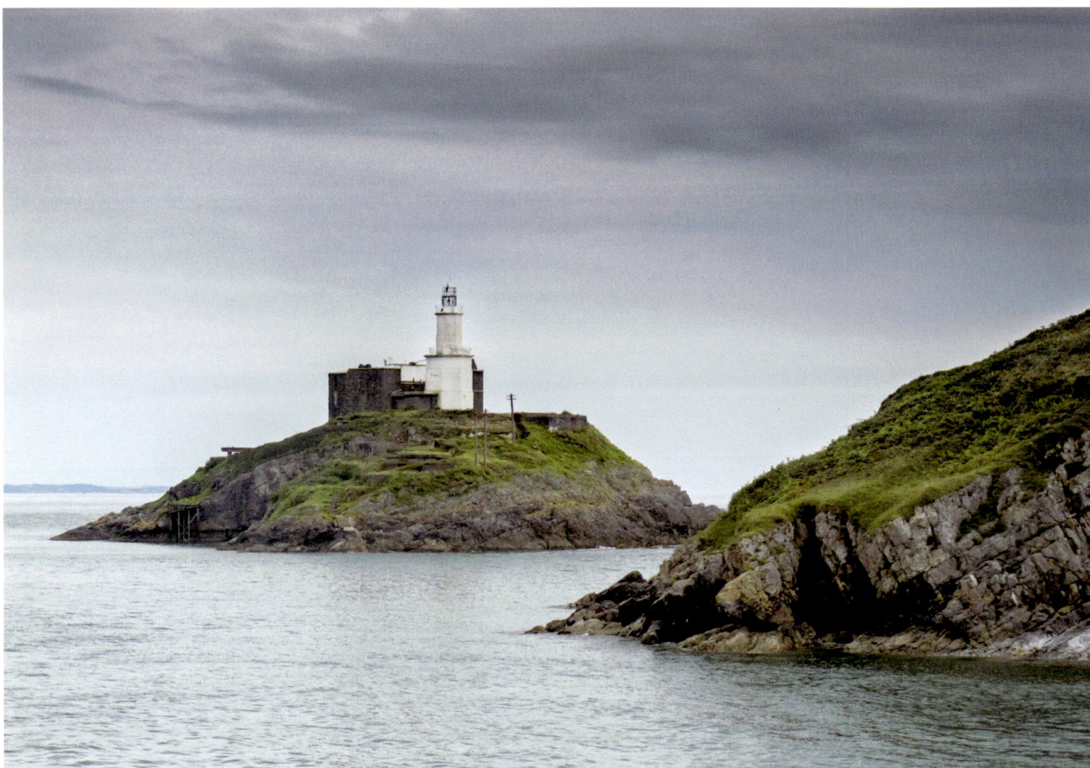

Mumbles Lighthouse. (© Chris Wakefield1, Flickr, CC BY 2.0)

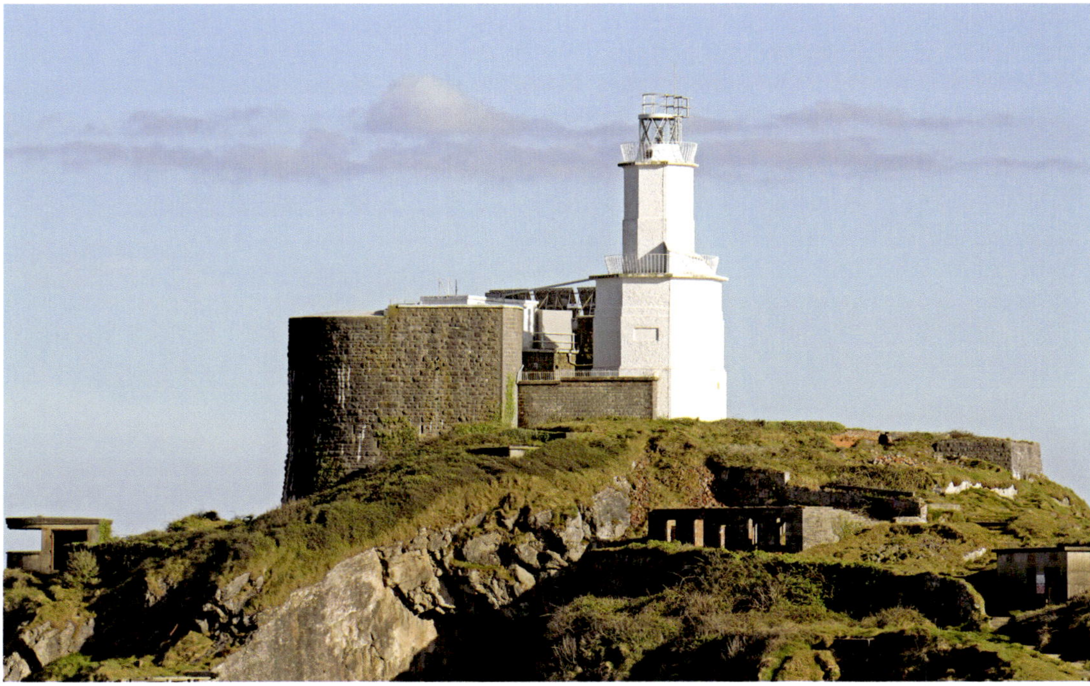

Mumbles Lighthouse. (© Tony Hisgett, Flickr, CC BY 2.0)

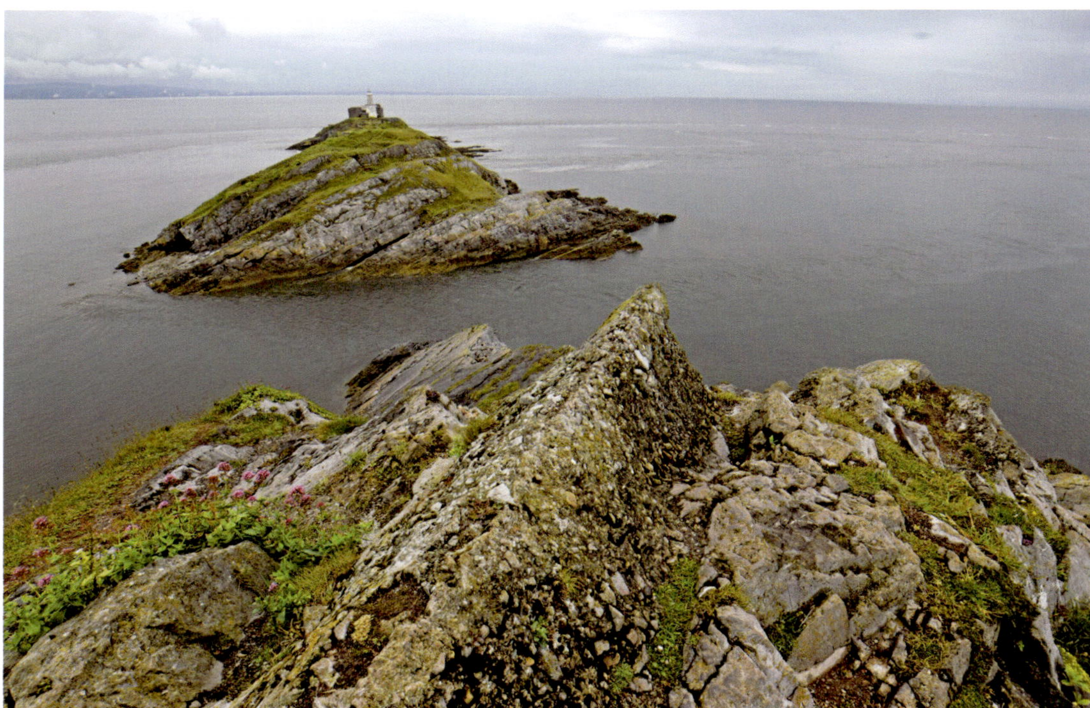

Mumbles Lighthouse. (© Mark Wordy, Flickr, CC BY 2.0)

Rejected by the Sea

In the eighteenth century, the Revd Edmund Jones recalled how an Englishman arrived in Swansea and caused a stir among the locals with his unorthodox religious beliefs. The man was a deist and, as such, his worldview was based on reason and rationality that dismissed the divinity of Christ. His 'blasphemies' divided the people of the town, and the pious were 'disgusted' that his 'corrupting' ideas were being taken seriously by some. He would, however, pay the ultimate price for his crimes against God – according to Jones at least – when he 'shot himself to death'. Those who took their own lives were denied burial in sacred ground, and it was agreed that his body should be disposed of far away from their homes to ensure he caused no more trouble from beyond the grave. They decided to fling him into the bay where the cold waves could carry him far away, but the sea, it appeared, also rejected the suicide, and returned his body to the sand. They tried once more and, when the ocean again declined him, concluded that if his 'unclean' body offended both earth and water, he would have to be buried right there where he lay, in the sand on Swansea Bay. Jones, quoting scripture, reminded the faithful that as his burial was so ignominious, the resurrection of his soul would be to certain damnation, and if any lost soul does walk the sands of Swansea, then this man would be a prime candidate.

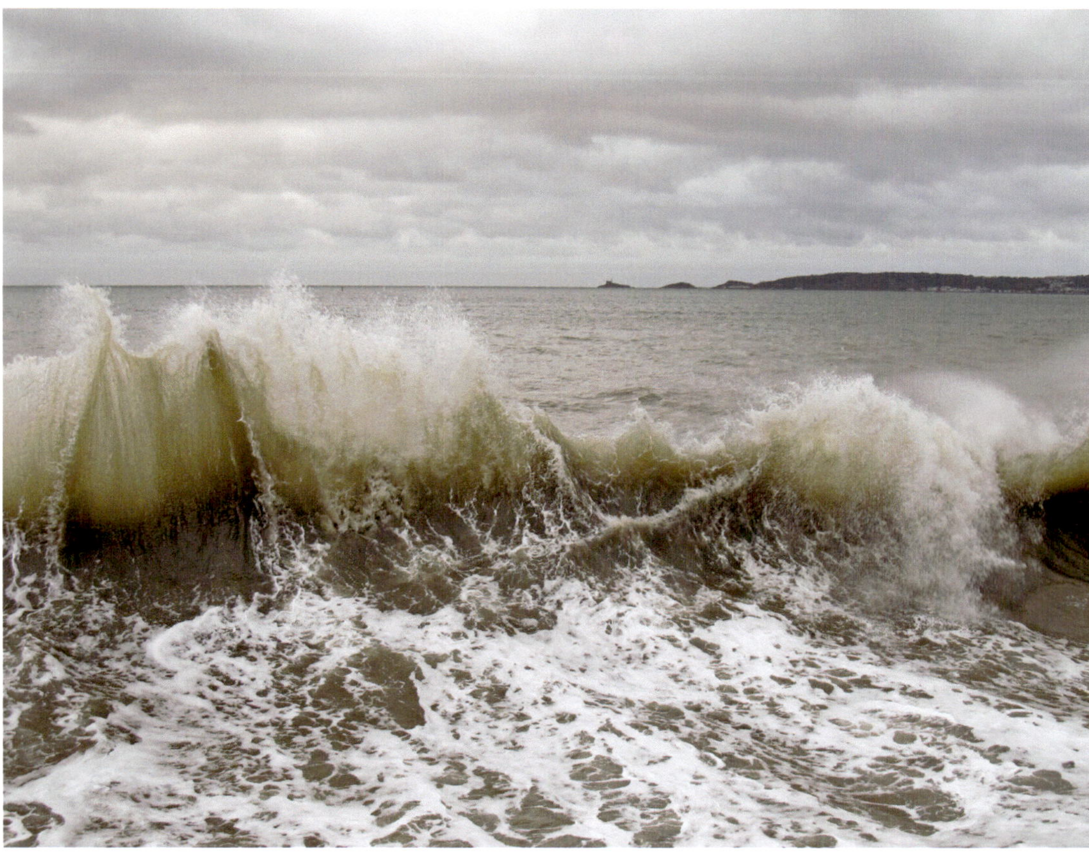

Rough seas in Swansea Bay. (© TruTourism, Flickr, CC BY 2.0)

Age of Copperopolis

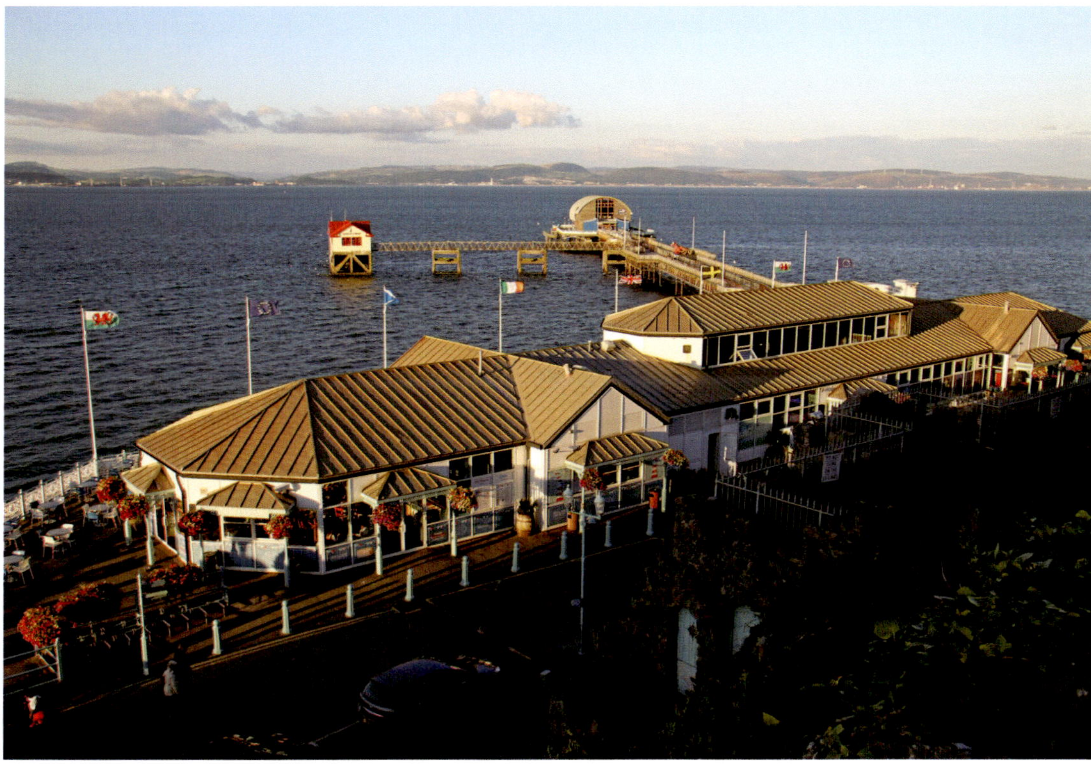

Mumbles Pier, a Victorian pleasure pier built in 1898. (© Steve Knight, Flickr, CC BY 2.0)

The Victorian age is described as the golden age of ghosts. In Swansea it was also the golden age of industry, with the then town becoming known as Copperopolis due to the vast quantity and quality of copper it produced. Advances in print technology meant that newspapers were more readily available than ever before, and editors were hungry to fill their pages with sensational tales of the supernatural. At the same time, the act of ghost hunting took on a more professional air, and in 1882 the Society for Psychical Research (SPR) was formed in London, the 'first organisation to conduct scholarly research into human experiences that challenge contemporary scientific models'. The SPR were active in and around south Wales, with future president H. H. Price hailing from Neath, and in 1893 made an appeal for information about the case of 'mysterious bellringing' in Loughor. The apparition of a 'little grey man' had been seen on two occasions at Ewbank Cottage where, try as they might, they could not stop the bells from ringing. They cut the wires and still they rang out, and when they stuffed the bells with cotton wool to mute the sound they swung about violently. As we shall see in this chapter, there were many more spirits haunting *fin de siècle* Swansea Bay, although some of them proved to be more genuine than others.

Swansea Séances

Spiritualism was booming in Victorian Britain. Anyone and everyone could commune with the dead like never before, with psychic mediums using increasingly elaborate techniques to answer questions from beyond the grave. Swansea established its own spiritualist community, although one local enthusiast bemoaned the fact that, despite being 'the most intellectual of the large towns in Wales', it did not fully embrace the movement like Cardiff and Llanelli. Circles, as groups of spiritualists are known, met regularly and recorded all manner of activity, from tables rocking to musical instruments being played by 'invisible agencies'. Captain H. Hudson, a prolific proponent of spiritualism and a prominent mesmerist, held packed weekly séances in St Mary Street where 'strong manifestations' were obtained. These circles were often joined by local and visiting mediums, such as Gorseinon-based miner Will Thomas who found fame as one half of the Thomas Brothers, the mediums who conducted a 'famous séance' in Cardiff that astonished Sir Arthur Conan Doyle, the creator of Sherlock Holmes.

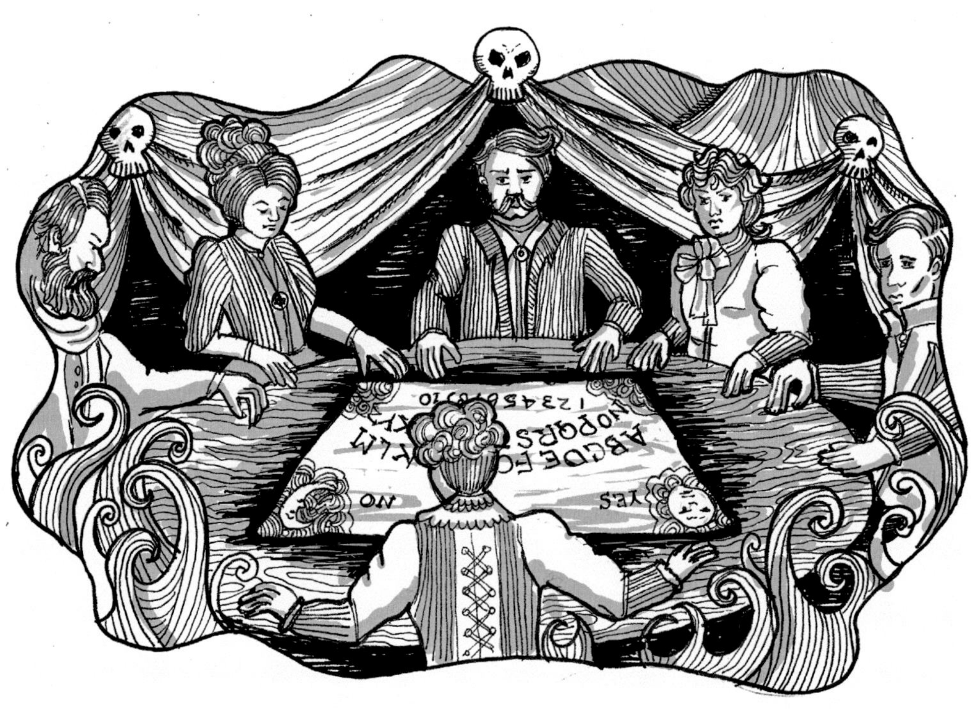

A Victorian séance. (Art by Sandra Evans)

For a first-hand account of a commercial séance in Swansea we can turn to a man named Clearstone, who visited a medium in 1879. He was invited by a friend and, curious to see what all the fuss was about, and seemingly keen to spend some time in the dark with a group of young ladies, decided to tag along. They headed for the parlour and, despite some of the 'maidens' having last-minute doubts, they found it to be a remarkably normal-looking room. The séance consisted of two halves, a light séance and a dark séance which, as the names suggest, were conducted in the light and in the dark. For the first half they sat with their hands flat on a round table and communication with the spirits was conducted by calling out questions and receiving thumps on the table in reply. The questions were generally light-hearted and concerned affairs of the heart, although the gallant spirit did spare a few blushes when asked such questions as 'Will it tell the ages of the ladies?'. The dark séance was a far more intense experience, and with the light extinguished they joined hands and sat in anticipation. Spectral chains clanked in the darkness, a floating tambourine bumped them on the head, and as the ladies shrieked a phosphorescent light danced around the room. The worst 'horror' was a cold and clammy hand with 'deathlike fingers' that searched for their faces. The experience was 'past human endurance', and when one of the ladies fainted the séance descended into chaos and ended abruptly.

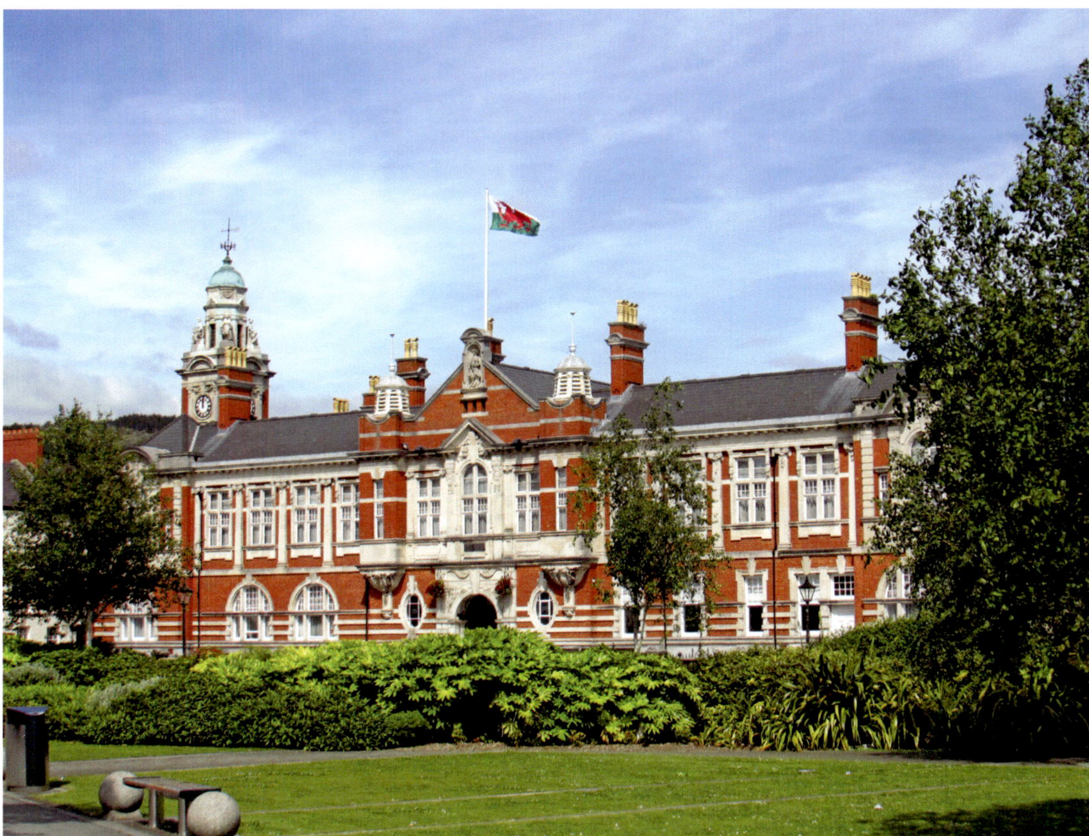

Victoria Road, near where the old Harbour Building stood; the hotel visible on the street is where the Harbour Building relocated to. (© Tom Bastin, Flickr, CC BY 2.0)

In 1876, a far more 'powerful' séance took place in which 'wonderful physical manifestations' were experienced in an apartment at the Sailors' Home in Victoria Road. Demolished in 1964, having stood next to the old Harbour Office which relocated to Adelaide Street in what is now Morgans Hotel, a large circle of eighteen people consisting of mainly 'earnest investigators' were led by the medium Willie Eglinton. The dark séance took place in a dining room with paper placed on the table in the hopes of receiving written communication from the spirit world. Little happened for the first hour and, in a bid to gain 'harmony' in the room, some people switched positions and, almost instantaneously, the 'manifestations' began. Chairs were pulled out from under several sitters including the medium and the author of the account, who claimed that he could also feel hands rummaging through his pockets and stuffing paper down his back. All but one participant felt 'spirit touches' on their bodies, 'beautiful lights' illuminated the room, and a music box weighing 7 lbs floated in the air and played tunes on demand. They discovered the spirit was a feisty character called Joey, and when a man asked him to write on the paper, he stuffed it in his mouth instead. The man responded by attempting to bite the spirit's finger, after which a seriously displeased Joey started violently hurling objects. The medium, concerned for their safety and with his powers waning, pleaded for calm and ended the séance. Afterwards, they inspected the paper on the table and among the many marks and scribbles found three decipherable messages: the words 'God bless you', the initials 'D. G.' which matched the name of one participant, and the name of their tormentor, 'Joey'. The affair was described as 'either convincing or mystifying'.

The Graveyard Ghost

In the late nineteenth century, a Mrs Phillips spoke with a reporter about some strange experiences that took place in and around her house in Swansea. She claimed to be 'associated with spirits' – hence the reason she attracted the paranormal like a magnet – and one night when home with her daughter they heard loud knocking on the kitchen window. They rushed downstairs to see what the commotion was when they encountered a 'ghost' that instructed Mrs Phillips in a 'mournful and solicitous tone' to 'go to bed'. She was in no mood to be told what to do by an intruder and made her feelings known in no uncertain terms, which only served to enrage the spirit. Its face transformed into a hideous visage with glowing red eyes and tusk-like teeth. She did not need to be told twice and dashed upstairs to bed.

On another occasion, her daughter was late arriving home, and Mrs Phillips went in search of her with a friend. They headed towards a house she was known to spend a lot of time at and, as they walked past Ebenezer Chapel, saw a figure wearing a grey cape with a strong resemblance to the girl coming towards them. Assuming it was her daughter, Mrs Phillips approached and put her hand on her shoulder, but as she did so the figure's head disappeared 'exactly like a Jack in the Box'. Before her eyes it transformed into mist and vanished into the chapel through the keyhole of the door. It was over very quickly, but Mrs Phillips later discovered that she wasn't alone in seeing a spirit at the chapel, and that a young cleaner had been chased around the graveyard by something similar. Mrs Phillips would leave Swansea soon after, but things went from bad to worse when her new home in Burry Port was targeted by a poltergeist.

Uncanny Wraith of a Murderer

In 1898, a seaman committed a 'terrible murder' in his home in Powell Street. While in bed with his young wife, Henry O'Neill, alias Price, became 'frenzied' and 'slaughtered' her 'in a most brutal fashion'. Soon after, before facing justice for his crime – in this world at least – he took his own life by jumping into the nearby canal. As shocking as these events were, life soon returned to some kind of normality in the street, and the house was reoccupied. A year later, however, 'strange happenings' were reported in several houses, and some of the locals believed they had seen the ghost of O'Neill. His spirit was said to walk the gardens at night, and as a result doors and windows were securely bolted, and the women and children feared going outside. One witness claims she saw O'Neill peering through her window, another that he touched her face as she was taking the washing in, while a young boy was 'rendered seriously ill' by the mere sight of him. It was suggested that the reason he haunted the gardens was because he had buried his wife's clothing in a particular place that now attracted his spirit. The woman who occupied O'Neill's former home laughed when she first heard her neighbours' fears, but an incident soon changed her mind. Having dug up the garden to lay a smooth surface, the next morning she found unaccountable footprints in the earth that led to that very spot. Afterwards, it was decided that a group of brave men should keep watch all night, but they were unable to catch the culprit. The local newspaper dismissively suggested they should 'bring a little common-sense to bear on the subject' and the mystery remains unsolved.

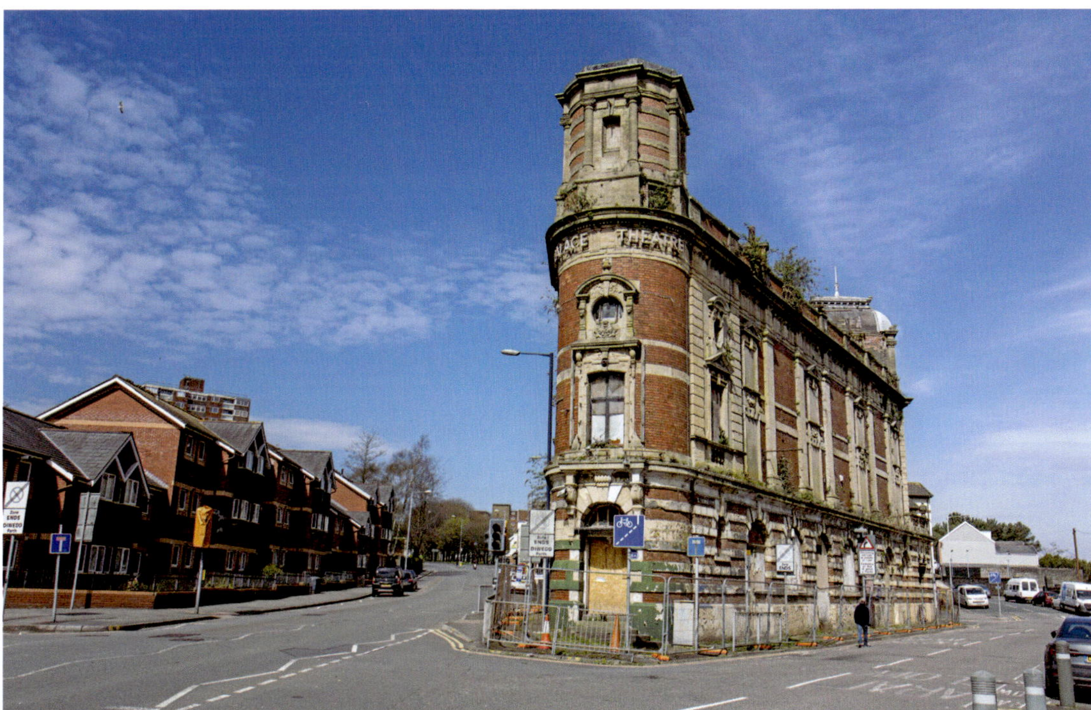

The Palace Theatre, around the corner from the now-demolished houses on Powell Street. (© Gzregozr, CC BY-SA 4.0)

Superstitious Miners

In a newspaper article appropriately headlined 'the Weird at Swansea', an unnamed 'Observer' recalled some of the superstitious beliefs held by the miners in their hometown. Mining was a major source of employment in industrial Wales, and it was understandable that those who risked serious injury or worse underground would be wary of anything even slightly out of the ordinary. Strange noises, smells and sights could be interpreted as ill omens that made them think twice about going to work that day. One of the worst disasters in the area was at the Morfa Colliery in Port Talbot where eighty-nine people lost their lives in 1890. This was the deadliest in a series of fatal explosions at what became known as 'The Pit of Ghosts', where the warnings included the ghost of a worker who appeared among the men as they travelled upwards in the cage, and a 'ghost dog' who raced off into the darkness ahead of a tragedy. Sometimes, it wasn't the miners themselves who had the premonitions, and the Swansea 'Observer' noted how a particularly psychic mother might stop her son from doing their job 'because she feels that something is going to happen'. There are also accounts of those who did not heed the warnings, such as a Swansea miner who woke one morning to see a blackbird on his bedroom windowsill. He thought it 'rather unusual', but not so unusual that he downed tools and went to work as normal. When he returned home with a 'smashed arm' that afternoon he realised the full significance of the 'omen'.

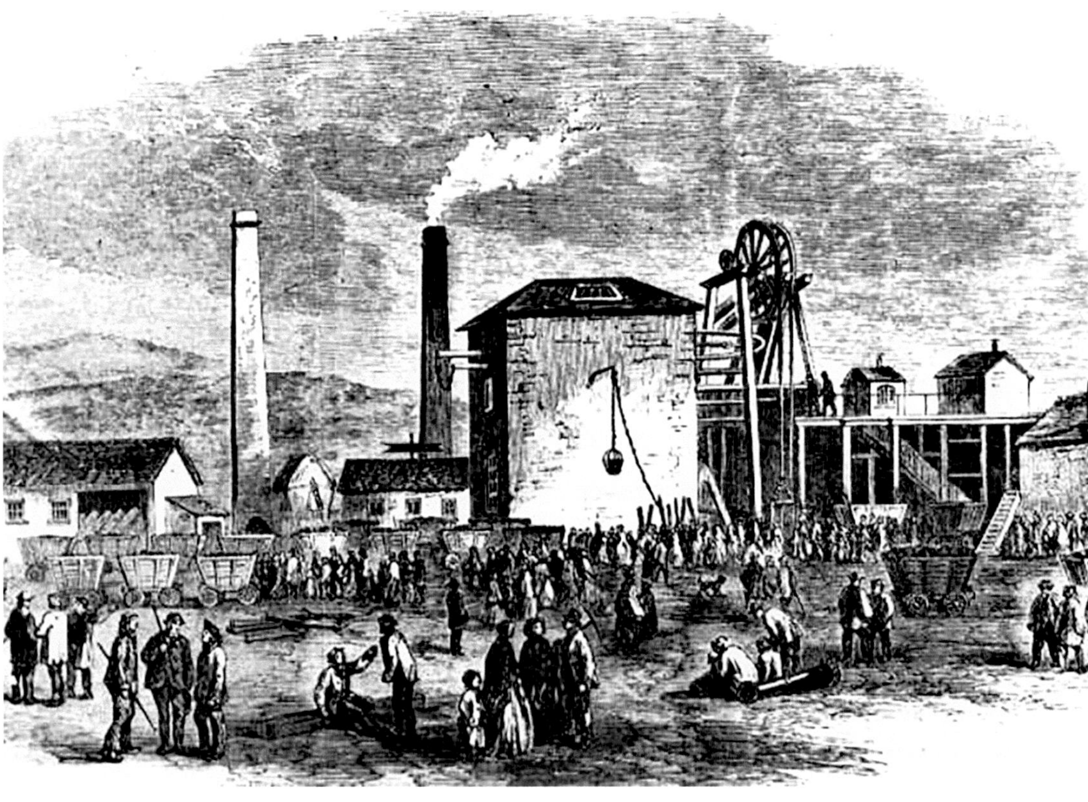

Morfa Colliery in 1863 shortly after the explosion.

A Ghost to Rival Hamlet's Father

In 1895, a ghost story broke that quickly became one of Swansea's most talked-about hauntings. It centred around a terraced house in York Street, and such was the media attention that hundreds of would-be ghost hunters flocked there to peek inside, banging on the front door, and even climbing the back wall. It all started at 12.05 a.m. one night when Caroline Bond, who lived with her husband but was home alone, was sitting in the kitchen. She heard 'a strange, rustling noise' as if someone was coming down the stairs, and was horrified when she turned to find 'some strange weird spectre standing behind her'. This spectre opened the back door and beckoned her to follow it out into the darkness, but Mrs Bond quite wisely decided to stay inside. With that, the ghost was gone – for now at least, anyway, because the 'unwelcome stranger' reappeared at the same time the next night. She had dismissed the previous visit as a trick of her imagination, but this time it left her shaking and frozen to the spot. Determined not to be caught off-guard a third time, she arranged for her husband, along with some brave neighbours, to sit with her in the kitchen the next night.

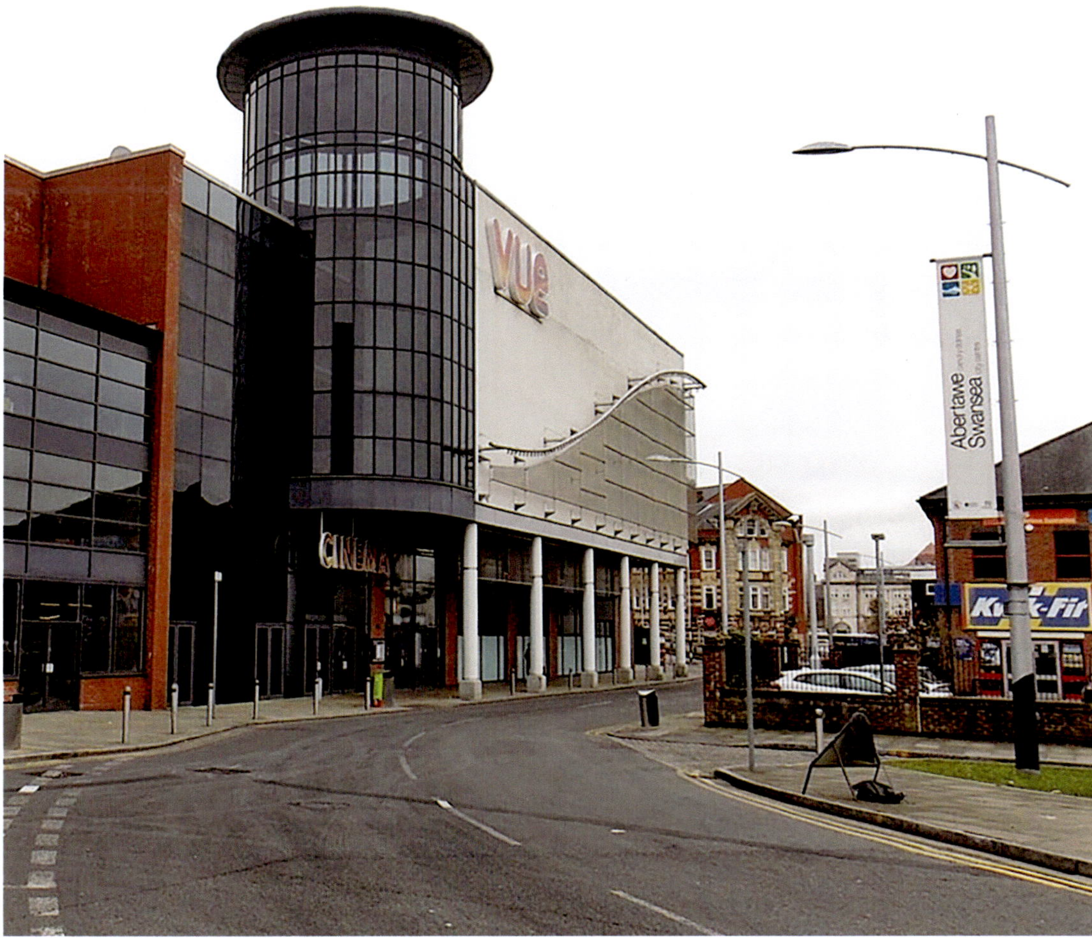

A view of York Street where the house once stood. (© Jaggery, CC BY-SA 2.0)

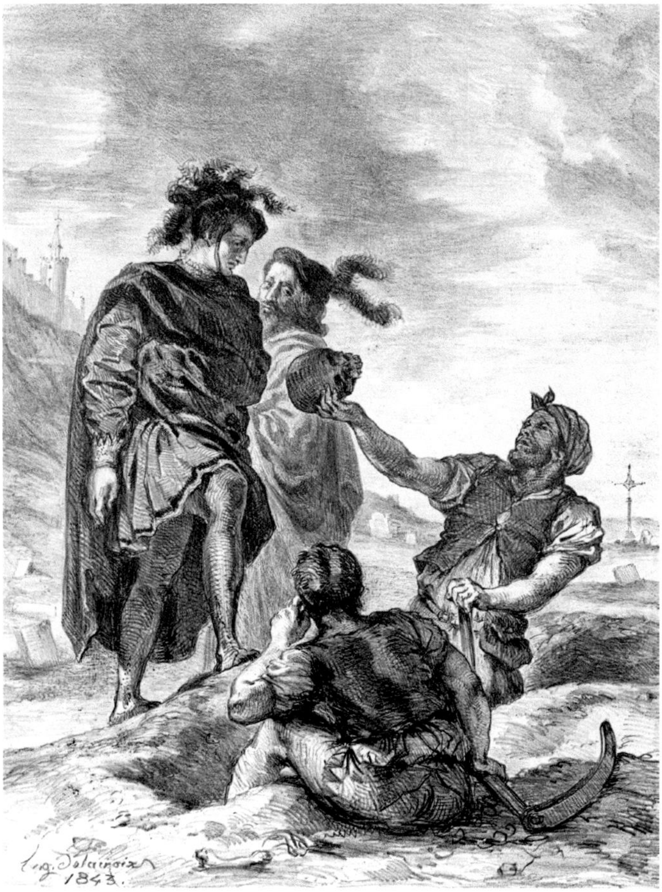

A nineteenth-century print showing the scene from *Hamlet* in which a gravedigger pulls the skull from the ground.

They waited until late, and the ghost finally signalled its arrival by tapping at the door. They watched in shock as it opened the back door and bade them to follow it into the garden, and this time they did just that. They were all transfixed, staring at the ghost who appeared to hover over a particular spot, and suddenly the ghost vanished and the spell was broken. It was suggested that maybe the ghost was trying to give them a message, and that the area over which they hovered was important for some reason. Two men picked up shovels and began to dig in that spot until one of them hit a solid object. He picked it up and held it aloft in the moonlight, declaring: 'a human skull! Great Scott!' This discovery led to the spirit being dubbed a 'ghost to rival Hamlet's father' in the press, and the skull was given to Swansea Police who were based in the former Guildhall, now the Dylan Thomas Centre.

Swansea went a little bit ghost crazy following the publication of the reports, but it all came crashing to a halt when the police examined the skull and discovered a crucial detail: it was not a human skull, but the skull of a dog. As such, it was concluded that the entire affair was a big joke, and when the reporter returned to the house for an explanation, he was greeted by giggling neighbours. The case was closed but it still begs the question, just because the skull belonged to a dog, does that necessarily mean it was a hoax? What if the ghost wanted them to find the dog's skull? And if so, for what reason?

Paranormal Hoaxers

In the winter of 1902, the workmen at Hafod Silver Works came under siege from a 'mysterious visitant' who bombarded them with bricks and stones. This 'mysterious black figure' hovered over the roofs at night and, try as they might, they could not catch them. Unusually for such a case, a meeting was arranged with the 'dreaded apparition', who specified that they would only meet in a dimly lit room, and that nobody should approach them unless summoned. They appeared at the meeting place with their face concealed by a turned-down hat and an up-turned coat collar and explained that they were looking for the right person to speak to. They beckoned each worker forward until they found the right one, and while it is unknown what transpired between the 'ghost' and the man, they shaved off their moustache afterwards in a bid to hide their identity and avoid being picked on again. The reporter covering the story suggested it was an elaborate joke designed by some of the workers to scare their now clean-shaven colleague.

Two years later, reports of a 'noiseless visitor' haunting Cockett saw a group of men band together to hunt down the offender. They set up a watch on Station Road and scoured the neighbourhood at night, checking gardens and fields while the women peered out from behind the curtains. One of the men who was carrying a revolver for protection – these were the days when firearms were taken on ghost hunts – opened

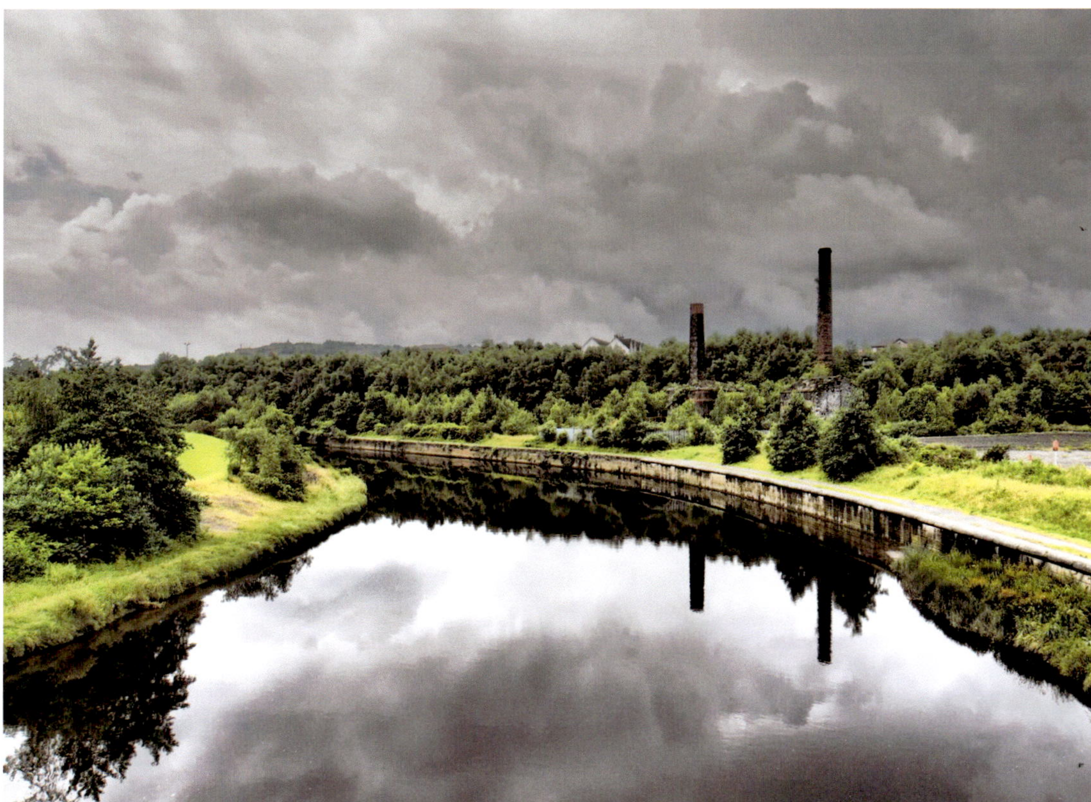

Remains of the Hafod works. (© Gareth Lovering, Flickr, CC BY-ND 2.0)

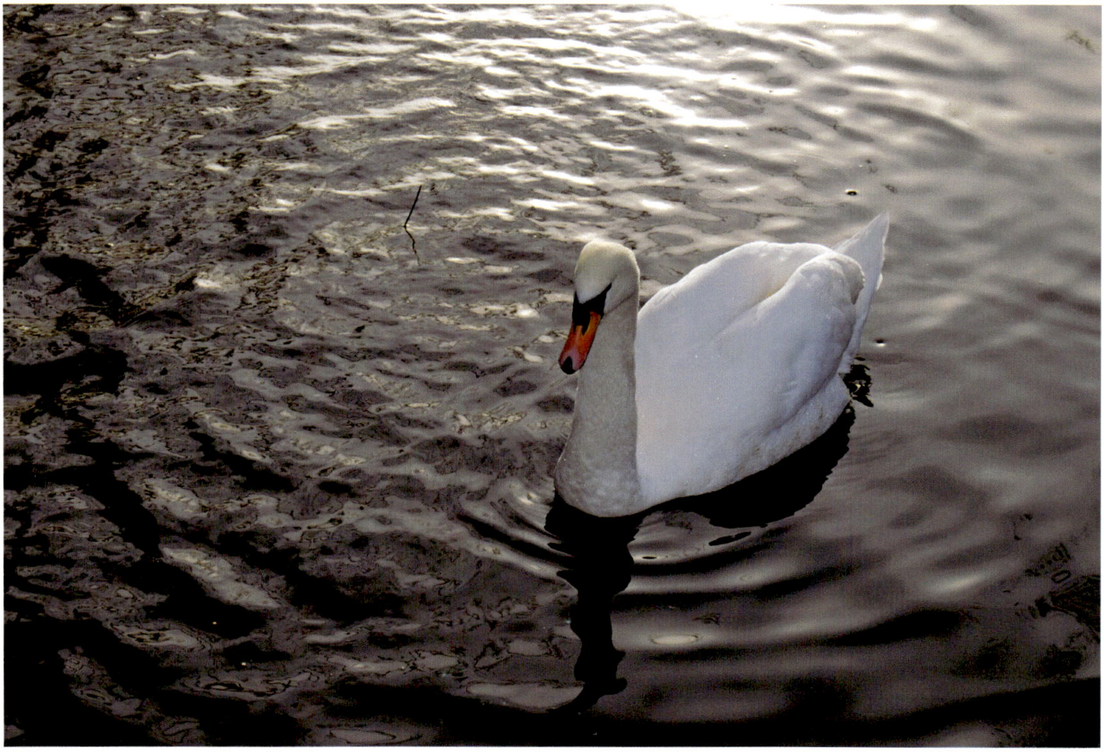

A Swansea swan in Brynmill Park. (© Chris Jobling, Flickr, CC BY-SA 2.0)

fire on an object seemingly moving by itself. His bullets hit nothing but the wind, and as a result a curfew was set up to stop anyone unfamiliar with guns from walking at night. The 'ghost' was known to have the ability to creep up on people without a sound, and when a man was found wearing shoes with 'silent soles' he became an instant suspect. Just like a ghost, however, he silently disappeared before they could question him.

In 1916, a rumour circulating among the youngsters of Brynmill claimed that a ghost could be seen on a particular street after dusk. As a result, a large group of increasingly unruly youths began to congregate in this once-peaceful part of town. The rumour, it was claimed, was started as a prank, and one local decided to put an end to this 'positive pandemonium' by throwing buckets of water on any ghost, or ghost hunters, who gathered outside his house.

The Caswell Ghost

The Caswell Ghost was first encountered in 1887 by an engineer who worked late-night shifts in Oystermouth. As he walked along the bay to and from work, he noticed a 'figure dressed in white, gliding along the road or flitting over the sands' that would suddenly disappear behind the rocks. While he insisted he was no coward, he admitted that the spook had given him 'many shocks' and vowed vengeance if he ever laid hands on it.

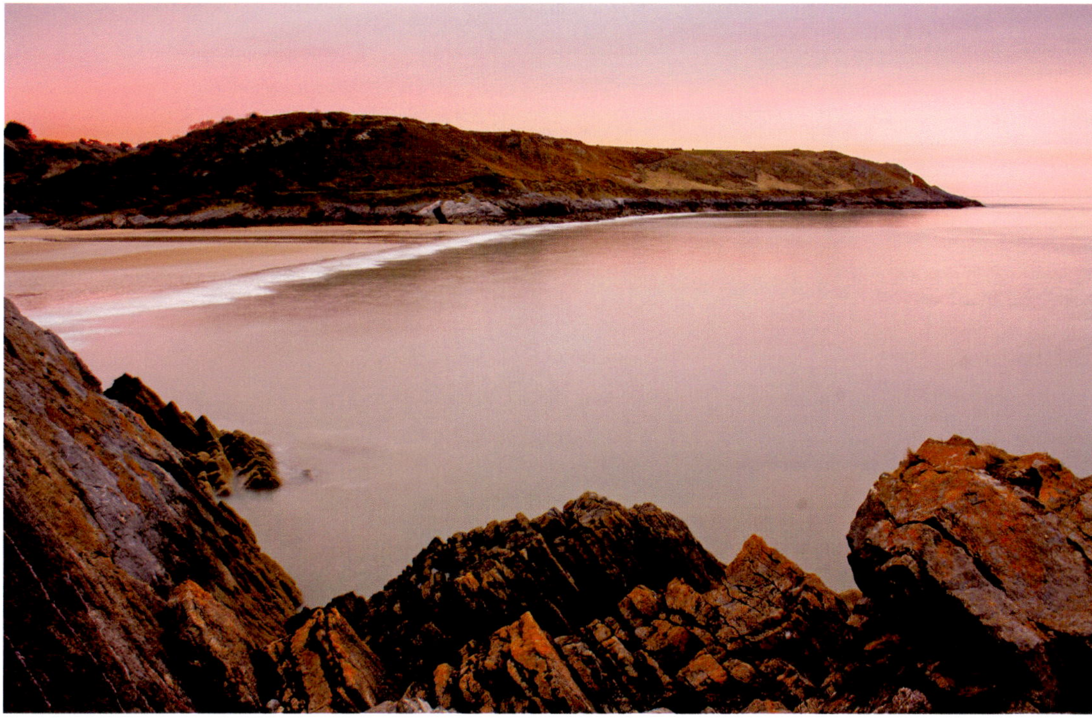

Caswell Bay. (© Catrin Austin, Flickr, CC BY 2.0)

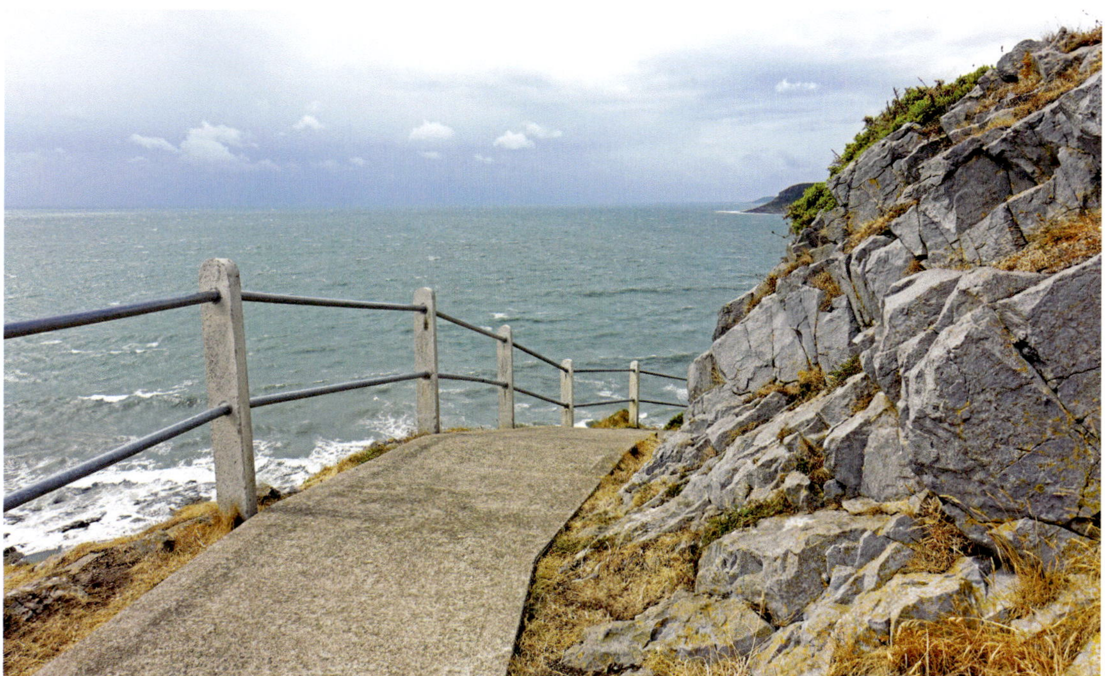

A path between Langland and Caswell Bay. (© Tiia Monto, CC BY-SA 3.0)

Things came to a head one Sunday night when a man in Newton heard a knock at his front door. Before he could answer the door swung open to reveal a figure dressed in white with a black face and arms. In a frightful voice it asked if it could have lodgings for the night, a request which left the occupier terrified and unable to speak. The form receded into the darkness, and when the man heard the garden gate click shut behind it, he snapped out of his daze. Realising he'd had a close encounter with the Caswell Ghost he rushed to his neighbour's house to warm him. After a quick shot of Dutch courage, the pair picked up weapons and set off in pursuit, which wasn't too difficult as the ghost had left a trail of children crying in its wake. They were joined by a third man along the way and bumped into Aunty Mary who told them she'd seen 'something queer' heading into the house of the old farmer Will Owen. The ghost repeated the same routine, startling Owen's granddaughter who answered the door, and when it asked for lodgings Owen answered with actions instead of words, swinging an oak staff at its head. Unusually for a supposedly ethereal creature, it ducked out of the way and made a hasty retreat, dashing into the street and right into the path of his pursuers. Aunty Mary shouted 'Catch hold of it and see what it is', but the ghost nimbly avoided a tackle and ran off down the road, only to encounter an even larger group of people – a congregation of mainly women leaving the evening church service. The ghost's effect on the startled churchgoers was absolute chaos; some fainted, some fled, and as their screams filled the air more people emerged from their houses. Their cries also alerted the vicar who looked down the hill to see a figure in white with a gang of men in hot pursuit. He joined the chase and, being a man of God who kept in shape, was the first to grab hold of the ghost. Shaking the suspect, he demanded: 'Speak, who are you?' In true Scooby-Doo style, one of the men pulled off his bonnet and revealed a face they recognised: 'Oh, my prophetic soul! *Will Warlow*.' It was a man familiar to many of the locals, and while the crowd wanted to enact vengeance then and there, the vicar insisted it was a matter for the police. Warlow, who is described as 'an otherwise steady and industrious man, civil and respectful in every way', pleaded that he was only trying to amuse his children.

Spring-heeled Swansea Jack

As some of these Victorian and Edwardian tales show, not all ghost sightings from this period were credible evidence of life after death. People impersonated spirits for all manner of reasons, from the more innocent pranksters looking to give a friend a good scare, to the criminals who used the paranormal to hide more sinister wrongdoings. One of the most famous examples who sits somewhere between these two extremes is Spring-heeled Jack, who initially made headlines for terrifying people in the south of England. One of Spring-heeled Jack's supernatural abilities, and the source of his name, was jumping great distances, with reports claiming that he easily avoided arrest by bounding away from the police. Over time he became more of an urban legend figure and started popping up all over the country, with reported sightings in Wales ranging from Wrexham in the north to Neath in the south. With a name like Jack, he naturally had to make an appearance in Swansea.

The Mumbles Spring-heeled Jack, as he was named, targeted people on Mumbles promenade after dark. He would lie in wait behind a bush or similar hiding place at around midnight until an unsuspecting victim walked past. With little street lighting the incidents happened in near total darkness, making witness reports vague, but the general theme was that he surprised them by leaping out of nowhere and laughing as they fled. He was, however, only active in the winter months, presumably because it is harder to hide during the balmy summer nights, until his reign of terror came to a sudden halt. It was New Year's Eve when he eventually picked on the wrong person, jumping out in front a burly docker who was walking home after a shift at Swansea Docks. Unlike the other victims, he did not run away but did the opposite, jumping towards his assailant and a scuffle ensued. The docker grabbed hold of Jack and dragged him to the nearest street lamp for a closer look. He was not surprised to discover that the ghost was, in fact, made of flesh and blood, but he was surprised that he recognised the face underneath the mask. It was a young man from Sketty who had made his way down the hill to scare the locals, and when he was asked the meaning of his 'strange antics' he claimed that 'It was only a joke.'

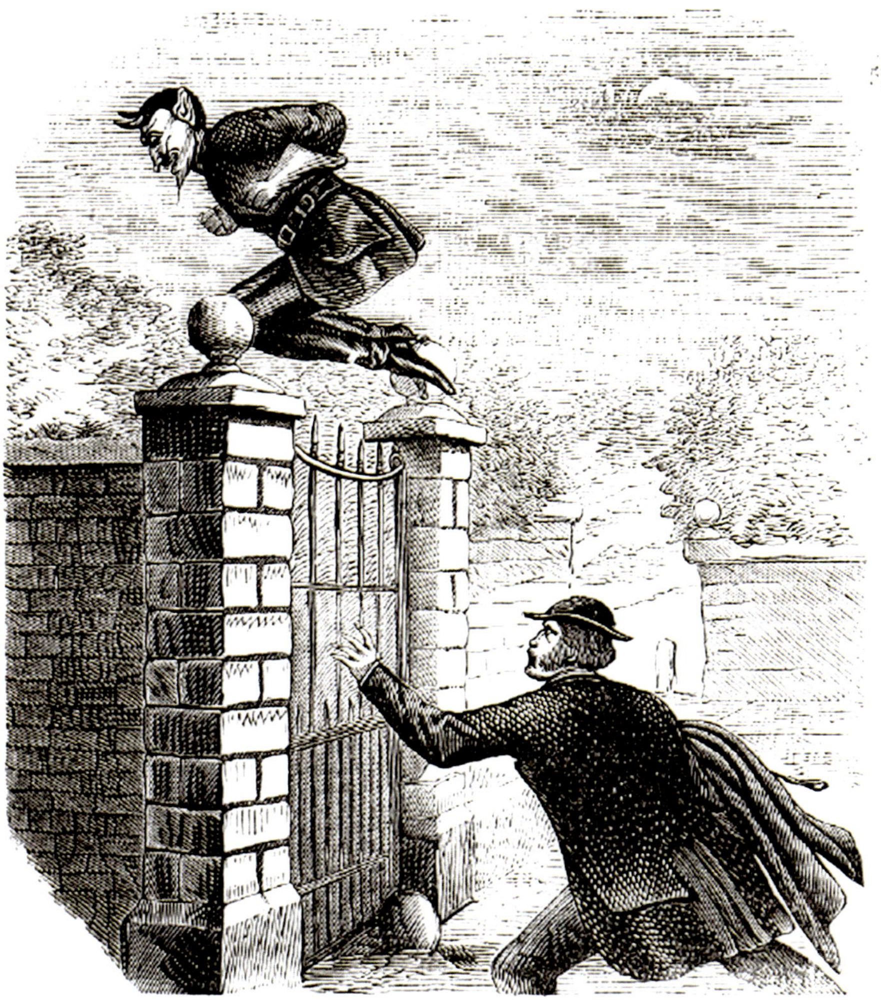

A nineteenth-century illustration of Spring-heeled Jack.

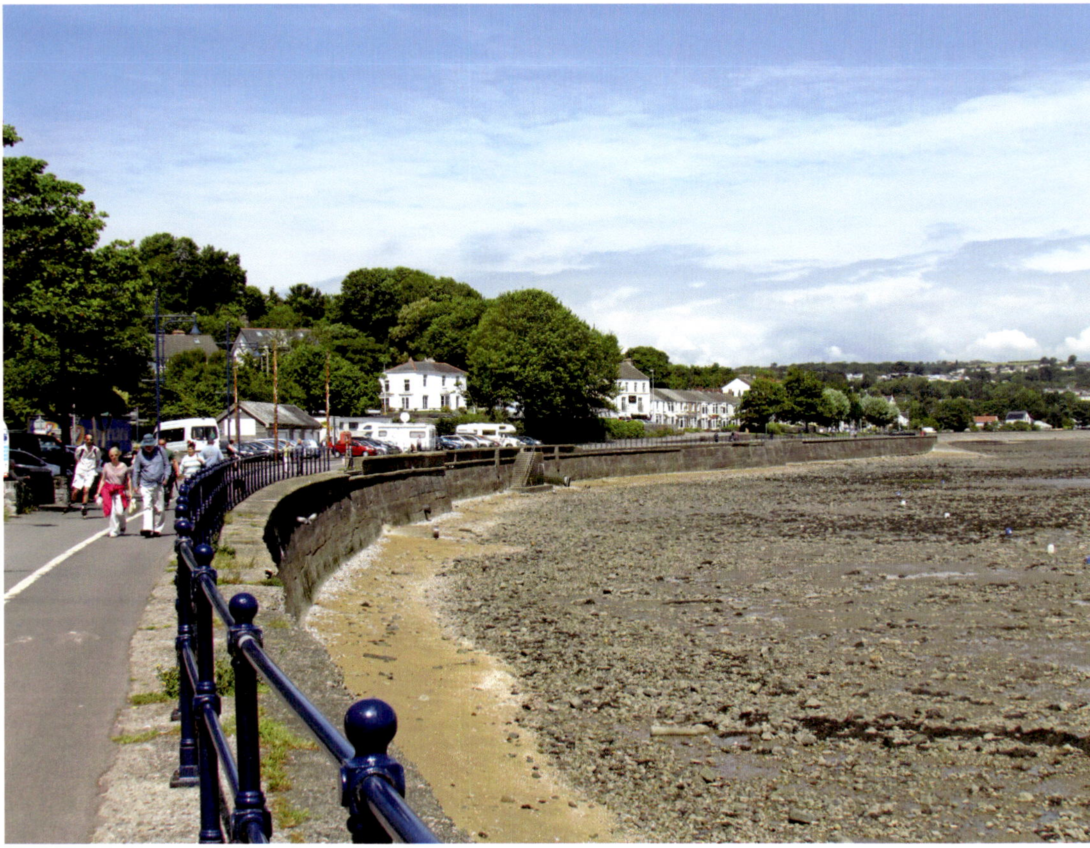

Mumbles promenade. (© Tom Bastin, Flickr, CC BY 2.0)

Modern-day Terrors

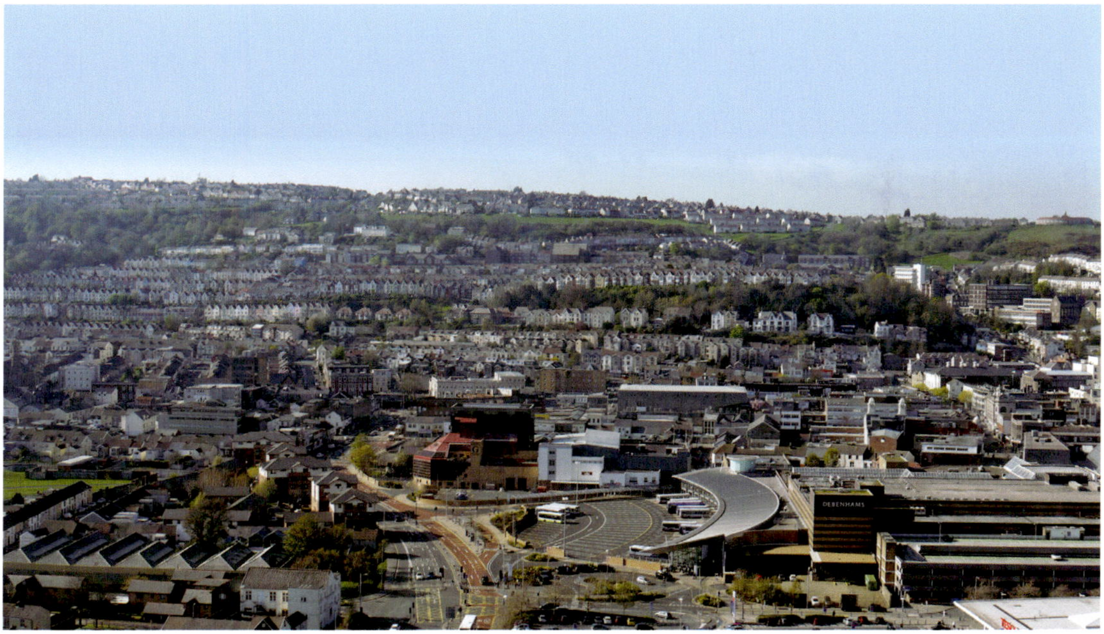

Swansea city centre from above. (© Malcolm Murdoch, Flickr, CC BY-SA 2.0)

In the twentieth century, new media and new technology brought new terrors to post-Industrial Wales. On the one hand, much of the ghostly – and not-so-ghostly – activity that shocked earlier generations was done away with thanks to such relatively innocuous advances as widespread electric street lighting. On the other hand, devices that allowed for sound and video to be recorded and environmental factors to be measured added greater credibility to those cases not so easily disproved. In this chapter we'll explore several hauntings from more recent memory, and the spirits that plagued our modern-day roads, workplaces, and homes.

Rhondda Street Poltergeist

In 1965, the press descended on Rhondda Street in Mount Pleasant for what was to become Swansea's most high-profile haunting in living memory. TV crews trained their cameras on the terraced home of the Howells family who had been forced to flee because, they believed, they were sharing it with a poltergeist. David, Marcia and their two young children, a daughter and newborn boy, found shelter with relatives, and a reporter filming live from the scene claimed the police were 'completely baffled' by events.

The activity began several months earlier, but it was only in hindsight that they suspected it might have been paranormal. Marcia recalled how three days after moving in the couple suddenly woke up unable to breathe 'as if something was choking us'. A few months later, she opened the living room door at around 5 p.m. and a medicine bottle levitated into the air and hurled itself at her. She closed the door quickly and heard the bottle smash against it, and when she reopened the door saw another bottle in the air ready to be thrown. She grabbed the children and ran outside to wait for her husband. When he arrived home, they found 'the place was turned upside down', with furniture and clothing scattered everywhere: 'It was terrible ... The couch, the TV, everything just thrown in the middle of the room.'

Two days later, at around 3 p.m., Marcia's mother, Glendora, who had a room at the house with husband Jack, was keeping an eye on the baby in the front room while Marcia collected her daughter from school. When she returned, she found her mother waiting on the doorstep, having also fled after hearing crashing sounds in the locked living room. Marcia forced her way in to find the room had again been turned upside down, and upstairs discovered her bedroom had also been targeted. What distressed her the most was discovering that the baby's cot had been hurled under the bed, claiming that 'if he'd been in it, he would have been killed'. By the time David arrived home the kitchen had also been 'chucked about', and at this point they decided to alert the police. This is also when Marcia became convinced they were dealing with something supernatural, because whatever was causing the damage was seemingly moving from locked room to locked room without being detected.

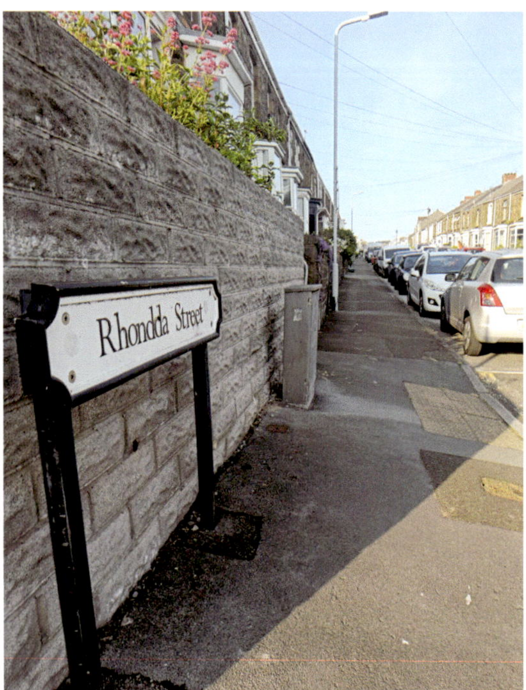

Rhondda Street. (Photo by Chris Carra)

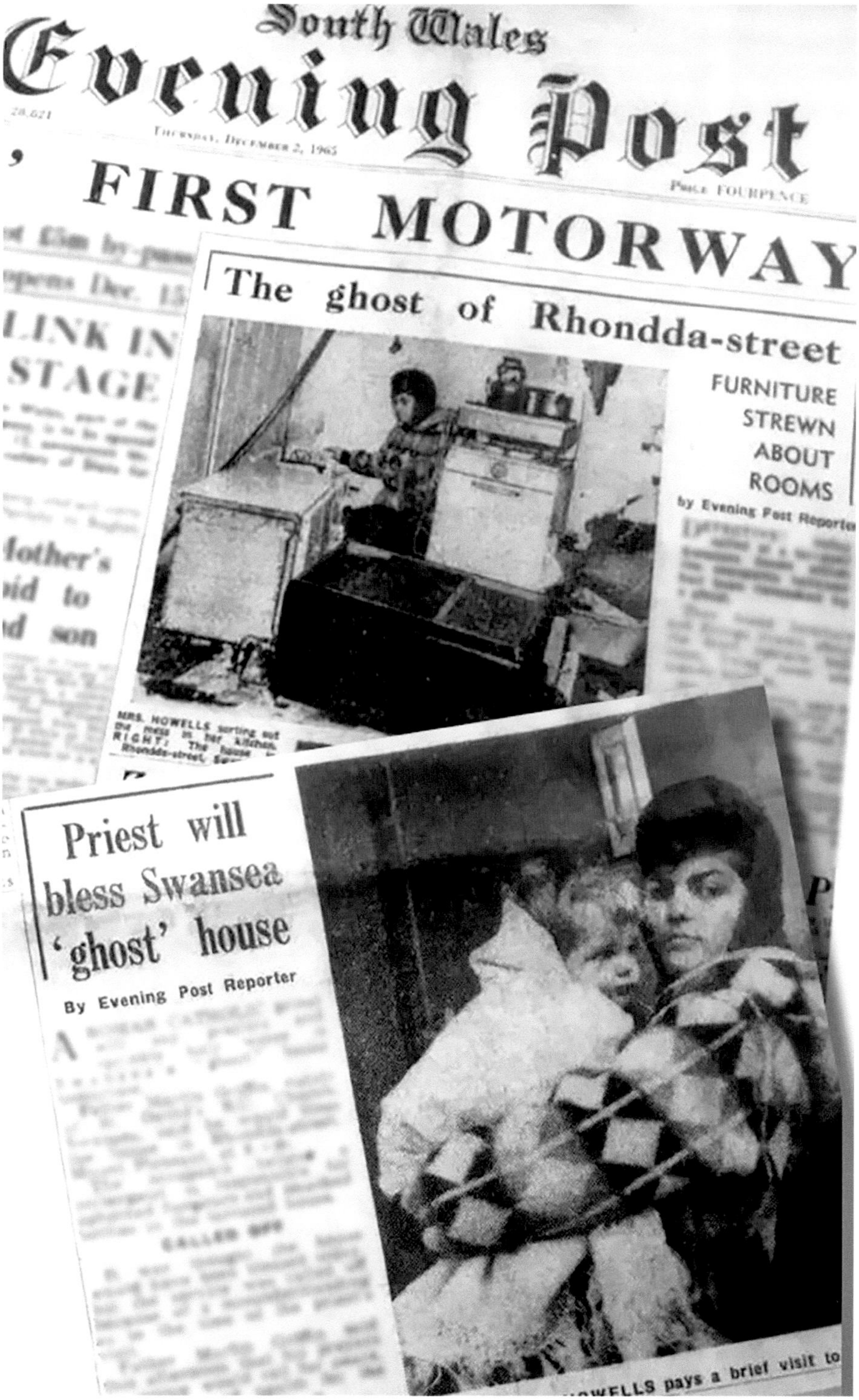

South Wales Evening Post

Thursday, December 2, 1965

Price FOURPENCE

FIRST MOTORWAY

The ghost of Rhondda-street

FURNITURE STREWN ABOUT ROOMS

by Evening Post Reporter

Priest will bless Swansea 'ghost' house

By Evening Post Reporter

Front-page news: 'The ghost of Rhondda-street' on the cover of the *South Wales Evening Post*.

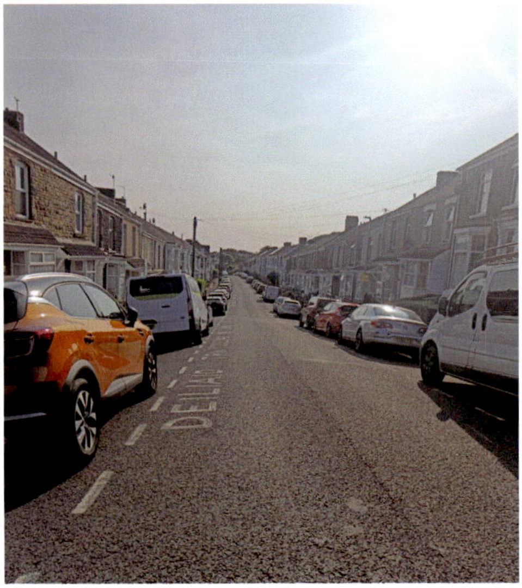

A view of Rhondda Street – long after the end of the poltergeist case. (Photo by Chris Carra)

The mystery attracted the attention of other investigators, such as Father Martin Griffin of St David's Roman Catholic Church and security officer Harry Homes, a 'psychic investigator' from Oxford Street, who could neither prove nor disprove the case. Alan Lloyd, a long-serving councillor, recalled the events in 2019: 'It was quite a story. People were talking about it, and some were very nervous. It was a different time, of course, and perhaps people were more naive then, but it caused quite a fuss at the time.'

When I spoke with Marcia in 2024, she remained convinced of the events as reported. She even revealed that she had turned down a sizable amount of money from a tabloid newspaper that wanted her to reveal it was a hoax. She has since dedicated much of her time to deepening her own spirituality and her spiritualist beliefs. Her daughter Beverley, meanwhile, who was too young to speak to the press at the time, also revealed a chilling extra detail: she can recall seeing the figure of a man at the end of her bed during the haunting. Describing it as 'a solid figure that seemed very real', it appeared to be wearing a hat shaped like a trilby.

Jersey Lil

In the winter of 1970, workers at the Ford plant in Jersey Marine were spooked by the sudden reappearance of a ghost who had not been seen since the days before the once-bustling complex produced car components. Jersey Lil, as the spirit was known, was something of a regular back when it was the Elba Tinplate Works, and several theories emerged as to her identity. One popular suggestion was that she had been a prostitute murdered while working in the nearby docks, and another claimed she was the victim of a rather gruesome workplace accident who died after falling into a pickling vat. Wherever she came from, she certainly had no qualms about where she went, and was first sighted at Ford in the toilets of the heat treatment area where a man felt a tap on his shoulder and turned to see her misty form. A similar figure was also seen descending the stairs in the main plant, although some believe it might have been an illusion created by the steam and smoke.

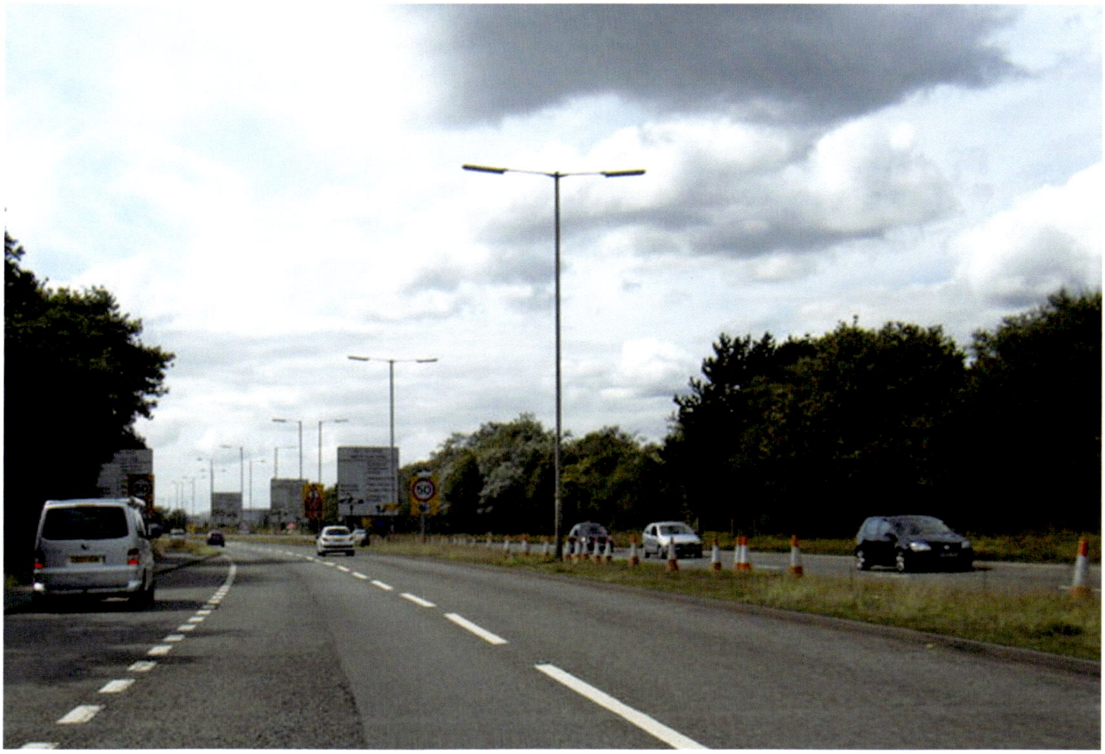

Westbound road near Jersey Marine leading towards the old Swansea Ford plant. (© Colin Pyle, CC BY-SA 2.0)

After reading the reports in the press, Geoffrey Hemming from Briton Ferry believed he had also seen the same spirit the previous year but this time outside the building. He and a friend were driving home after a late night out in Swansea, and as they passed the works they both saw a woman coming from the docks on the opposite side of the road. She walked directly in front of them as if she was on her way to the plant, which forced the driver to swerve to avoid hitting her. They ended up in the grass embankment and fearing the worst dashed outside to see if she was OK. They found no sign of anyone and assumed it had been a trick of the light, but after reading the newspaper he now believed it was Jersey Lil.

Phantoms of Penllergare

For more than two centuries, Penllergare House was home to the Price family, until a series of successions saw it become the residence of John Dillwyn Llewelyn, a Victorian photography pioneer whose sister Mary was the earliest known female photographer in Wales. While only ruins remain today, the vast estate on which the grand mansion once stood is now a popular visitor attraction. A haven for wildlife with rolling woodland and a spectacular waterfall, Penllergare Valley Woods is an idyllic place to visit during the daytime, but after dark, some say that it takes on a more supernatural atmosphere.

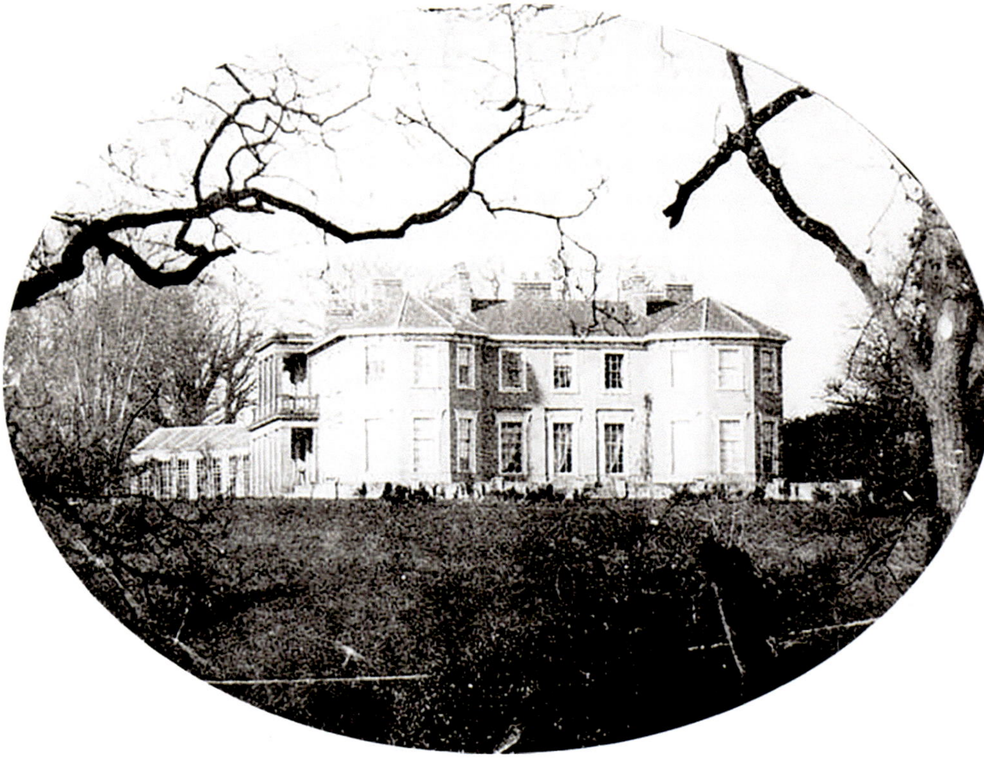

Penllergare House *c.* 1852. (John Dillwyn Llewelyn)

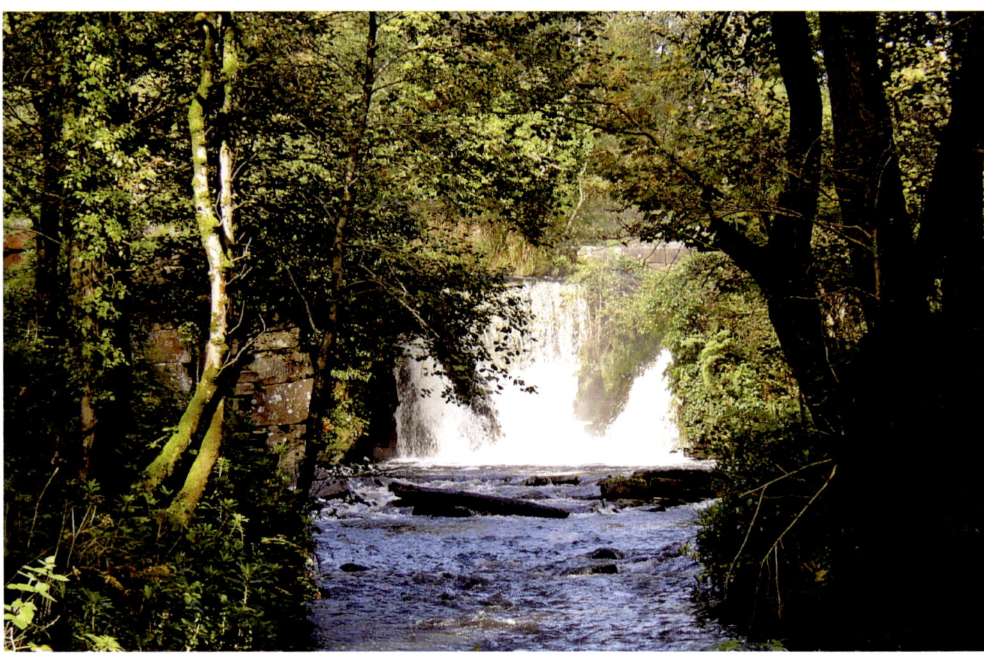

The Penllergare Estate waterfall. (© John Bristow, CC BY-SA 2.0)

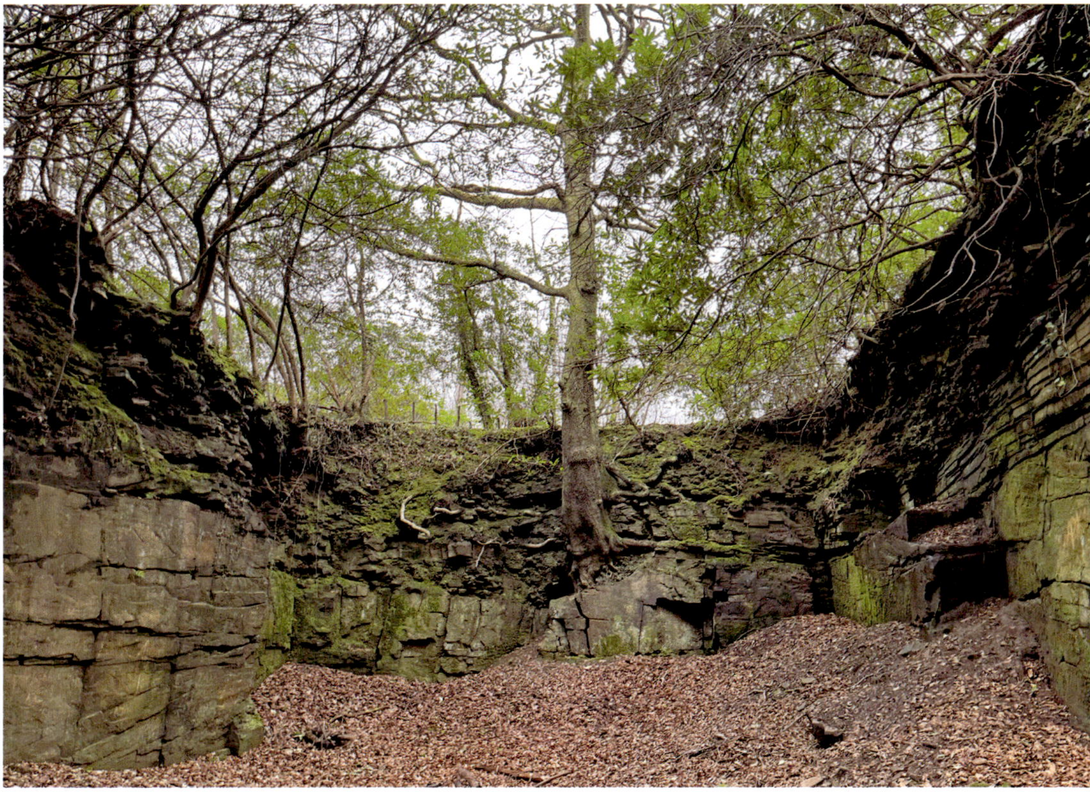

Exploring Penllergare by Jodie Williams.

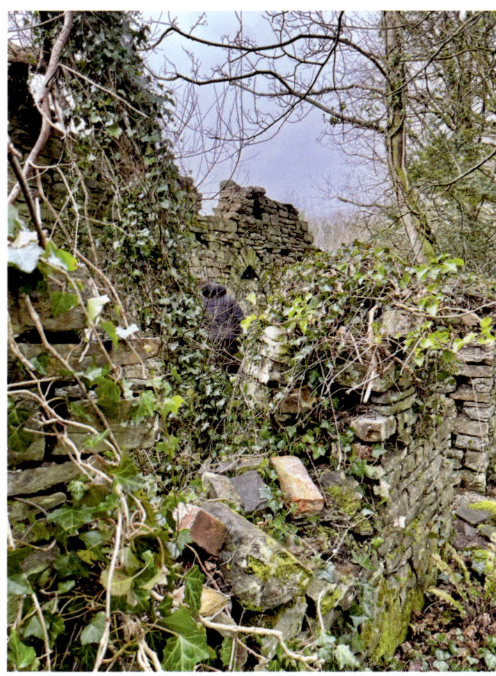

The ruins at Penllergare by Jodie Williams.

Reports of a haunting first began when the house was still standing. The industrialist Sir John Llewellyn, who was buried in nearby St David's Church in 1927, was so afraid of the figures that floated around the rooms that he wouldn't venture into the cellar alone. In more recent times, the paranormal activity has been focused on the grounds, where dogs cower as if from some unseen presence, and sudden blasts of icy cold air freeze people unawares. One tale tells of a grandfather and granddaughter who noticed a girl while walking through the bluebells near an old farmhouse. She was crying with her head in her hands, and as the sun's rays shone down through the trees they also went straight through the girl's ethereal body. Another speaks of a young man who arrived breathless at a local tavern one misty night. He had been walking through the woods when he heard footsteps following him at the same speed. Assuming it was an echo he stopped, but the footsteps continued. He then heard a horrifying snarl and ran as fast as his legs would carry him. While he never saw his pursuer, it left some evidence behind in the form of hoof marks in the grass.

One local investigator who visits the woods regularly is Joanne Williams. She is very much aware of a 'presence' in the area and says that several people have experienced the feeling of being watched as if by invisible eyes. There is one spot by the lower lake where 'you can definitely feel that there's things out there looking at you. You're always thinking, "who's behind me?"' She says this feeling is a form of intuition that experienced investigators will be familiar with: 'If you're used to ghost hunting you know that feeling, that change of energy.' She also singles out another area of interest that has long been believed to be haunted: a gravel driveway that once led to the mansion. Back in the house's heyday horses and carriages would have been a regular sight along this path, and it would appear they might still be seen and heard today.

Blasts from the Past

A man who was driving eastwards from Carmarthen in torrential rain lost all sense of direction after turning off the A48 near Penllergaer. He crawled along desperately trying to find a sign that might offer a clue as to his location and noticed a man in his headlights. He slowed down and, while he could not see the man clearly with his soggy hair hanging over his face and his collar turned up, he asked if he could direct him back to the main road. Without a word the stranger opened the door, sat in the passenger seat, and pointed ahead. The driver followed his instructions and they passed several landmarks including a church, and when he'd finally regained his bearings the stranger exited the car at Cadle Mill in Blaen-y-Maes. Days later, the man was driving the same route in much better weather and decided to take the shortcut the stranger had shown him, but when he turned off the A48 he could find no sign of it. He stopped for petrol and asked for directions to this road and was told that while they knew the road he spoke of, there was no way he could use it – it was closed years ago. Had he driven along a ghost road?

In earlier times, a nearby stretch of common land that the A484 now runs through also had a reputation for spooking travellers. One man who was crossing Garngoch common on horseback noticed a low breeze in the grass that appeared to be scaring his steed. As he neared Bryn Dafydd the wind increased in ferocity and the horse's fear grew until they stopped for a break at Afon Llan. As the horse drank from the river, the traveller noticed that its hooves were covered in what appeared to be blood,

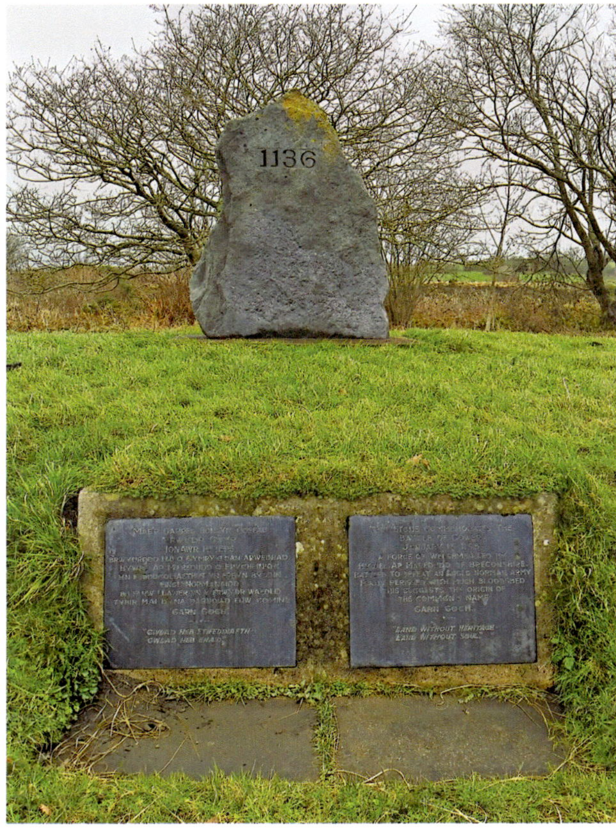

Commemorative stone at Garngoch. (© RhedynCochion, CC BY-SA 4.0)

which washed away as they walked through the water. Another man making a similar journey in a cart had a more terrifying experience when the wind grew so strong it forced him to huddle in his wagon. He heard what sounded like drums and then the battle cries of some invisible army and decided to make a run for it, regardless of the weather. Possibly unbeknownst to the traveller, this is where the 'Battle of Gower' between the Normans and the native Welsh is said to have taken place on New Year's Day in 1136. The Welsh were victorious, but more than 500 men from both sides lost their lives that day, their bodies 'horribly scattered among the fields and eaten up by wolves'. In 1986, a memorial stone was erected on the site that explained the area was named Garn Goch (red cairn) because 'many perished with much bloodshed'. Perhaps it also explains the origin of the haunting.

The Haunted Road

In 2001, a survey of the 'UK's top 10 haunted highways' was published in *Fortean Times*, the magazine devoted to 'the world of strange phenomena'. When speaking to the BBC about the survey, editor Bob Rickard explained that they had been inundated with reports of mysterious activity on British roads for years, and that it was 'clear that some ghostly sightings are being seen over and over again'. Two of those 'haunted' roads were in Wales, both of which involved spectral white ladies, one

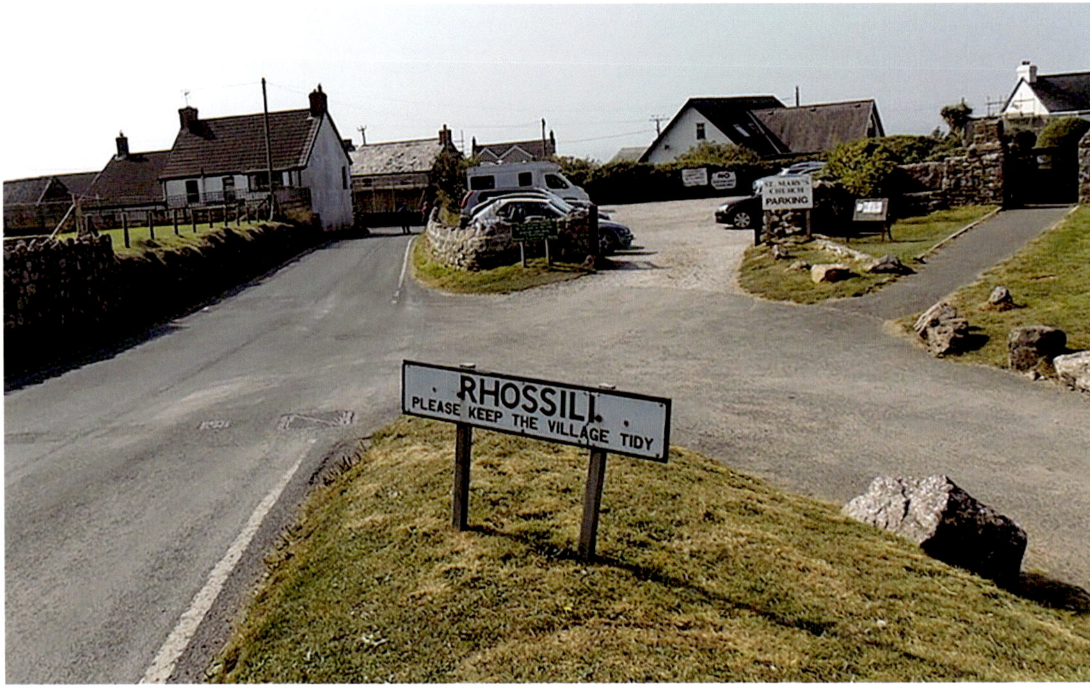

Welcome to Rhossili. (© Jaggery, CC BY-SA 2.0)

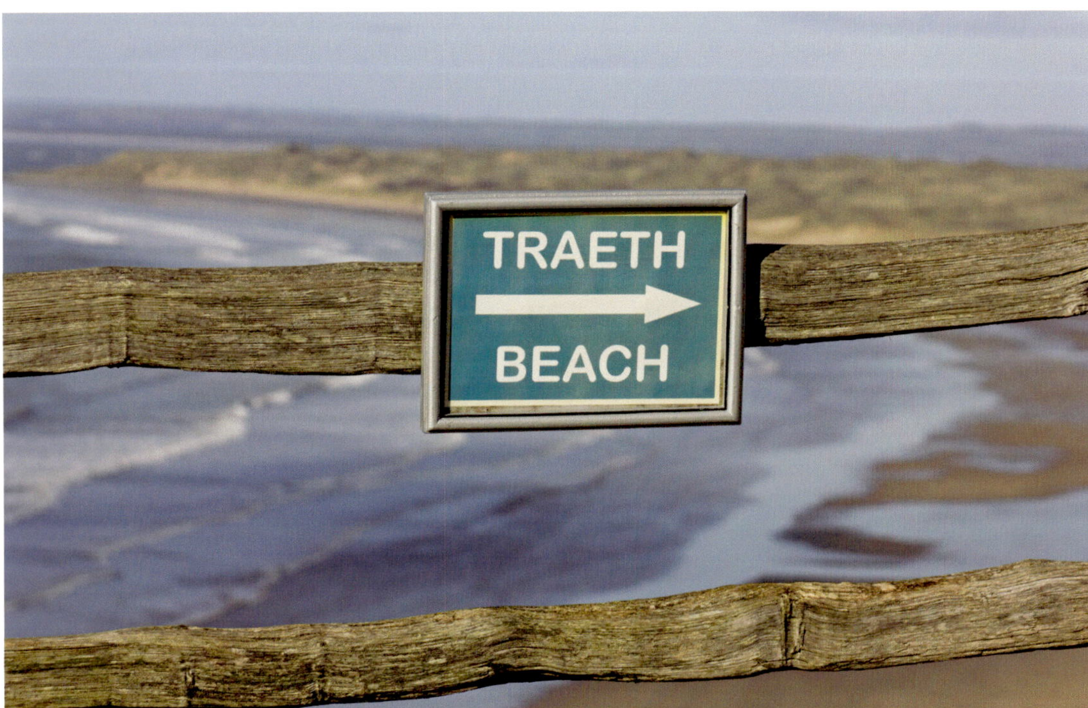

Clear directions to Rhossili Bay. (© Jeremy Segrott, Flickr, CC BY 2.0)

of which was in St Athan, and the other was in Gower. In the article, Paul Devereux wrote of how a surfer known as CP was making his way to Rhossili to catch the waves at approximately 6.30 a.m. He was driving slowly to avoid disturbing the locals so early in the morning, and it's lucky he was, or he might have hit, or maybe passed through, an unexpected obstacle. As he drove along the main road, which is assumed to be the road that cuts through the village before turning onto Moor Land and down to the sea, he saw a transparent woman dressed head to toe in white standing before him. She disappeared as quickly as she had appeared, and afterwards CP said that he knew nothing about reports of such phenomena. Devereux noted that 'his encounter had been on a stretch of road close to an ancient holy well, a typical location for this type of apparition'. Another unconfirmed sighting of unexpected creatures in Llangennith in the 1990s was presumably not paranormal, but it was certainly surprising: koala bears.

The Bed-flipping Phantom

The home of Revd David Phillips on what is now Hanover Street was once the scene of some rather unusual poltergeist-like activity. Whenever his back was turned, items of furniture would mysteriously move around the house. And not just small, easy-to-move objects; chests of drawers walked by themselves, and his bed repeatedly flipped itself over. The Methodist minister, who was described as a shrewd man who would not be deceived easily, could find no explanation for this activity, and began to suspect that evil forces might be at work. It soon became a daily occurrence and escalated to include weird noises, doors opening and closing, and even chairs flying around the room as if flung by unseen hands. Visitors to the house also heard objects being moved that sounded as if somebody was dragging them, but nobody was ever caught in the act. Fortunately for the reverend, the activity dwindled with time, as if the spirit was slowly running out of power. Unfortunately for us, the entire case remains a mystery as a result.

The Reverend's Haunted House

Another unusual tale concerning a reverend's haunted house was recorded by Russell Gascoigne and took place in Mumbles. It was in the 1980s that local hospital chaplain Revd Borthwick bought his new home on Tichbourne Street and was surprised when his neighbours told him that the previous occupant believed it to be haunted. While neither he nor his family ever saw a ghost, he did believe that there was a masculine presence sharing the property with them. They heard footsteps moving around the house, and tricks were played such as lights being turned on and off and windows being opened in the winter. On one occasion, a visitor dreamt of being drenched with cold water, only to find themselves soaked when they awoke. The house was a sturdy building roughly three centuries old, and the reverend believed that its history might shed some light on the ghost's identity. One potential culprit was a blacksmith who had lived and worked there and, it would appear, continued to return to his former forge from beyond the grave. Whoever the ghost may be, the reverend was not alarmed by their presence and was in no hurry to have them removed, especially when

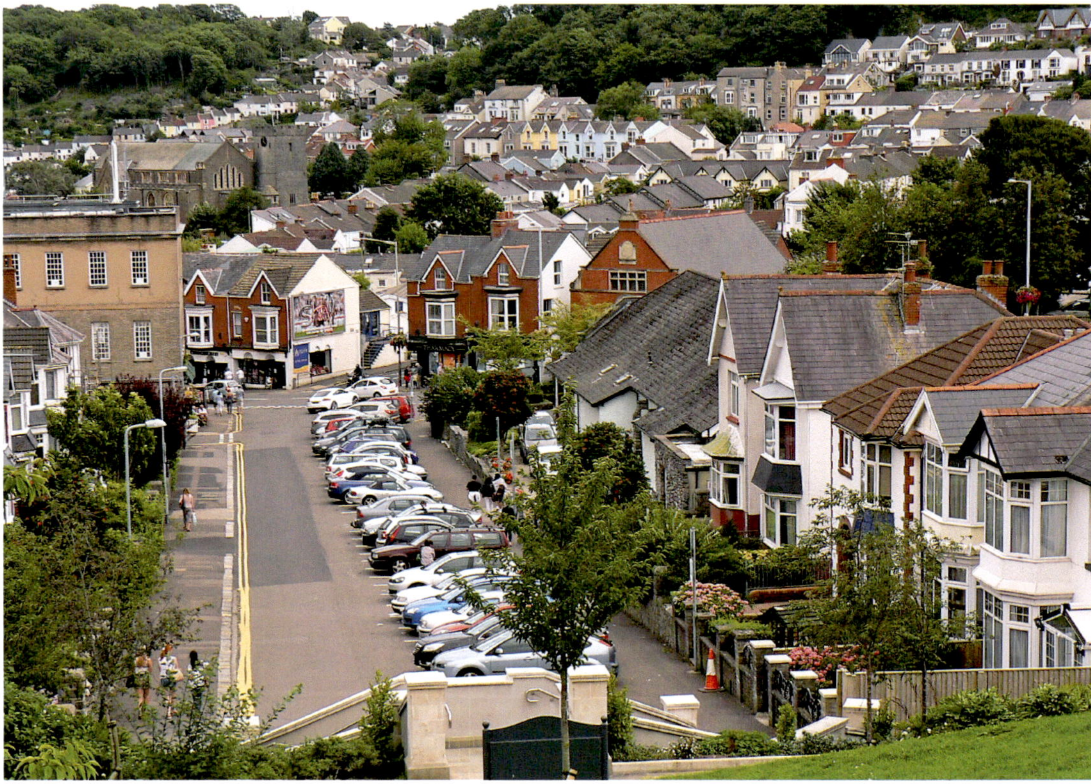

A view of Mumbles from Oystermouth Castle. (© John Bristow, CC BY-SA 2.0)

he accidentally discovered that it could perform party tricks. After asking aloud for the spirit to turn on the TV so they could watch the rugby, they did just that.

The White Lady of Pwlldu Bay

The White Lady of Pwlldu Bay has been described as a 'ghost that is not a ghost', which is a very apt way of describing an apparition that is almost certainly not paranormal but has surprised a few unsuspecting victims over the years. The name Pwlldu is Welsh for Black or Dark Pool, a rather ominous name for a bay that also contains a gully called Grave's End. Encircled by rocks, it is said to be the burial site of some sixty-eight people who died during the wreck of the *Caesar* cargo ship in 1760, although another location nearer Caesar's Hole can also lay claim to that title. Either way, a 'ghost' has been seen here by many people in the middle of the stream that leads to the ocean. It always appears at night in the same location, and this consistency has allowed the mystery to be solved. When the same spot is viewed in the daylight, a rock can be seen sticking out of a spring that flows over the cliff. On a cloudless night with the moon in the sky, its silver beams rebound off the water and onto the rock, giving it an ethereal appearance that might be mistaken for a ghost. It should be noted that this only applies on moonlit nights; if you encounter a spirit in Pwlldu Bay when there is no moon in the sky, it might not be an illusion.

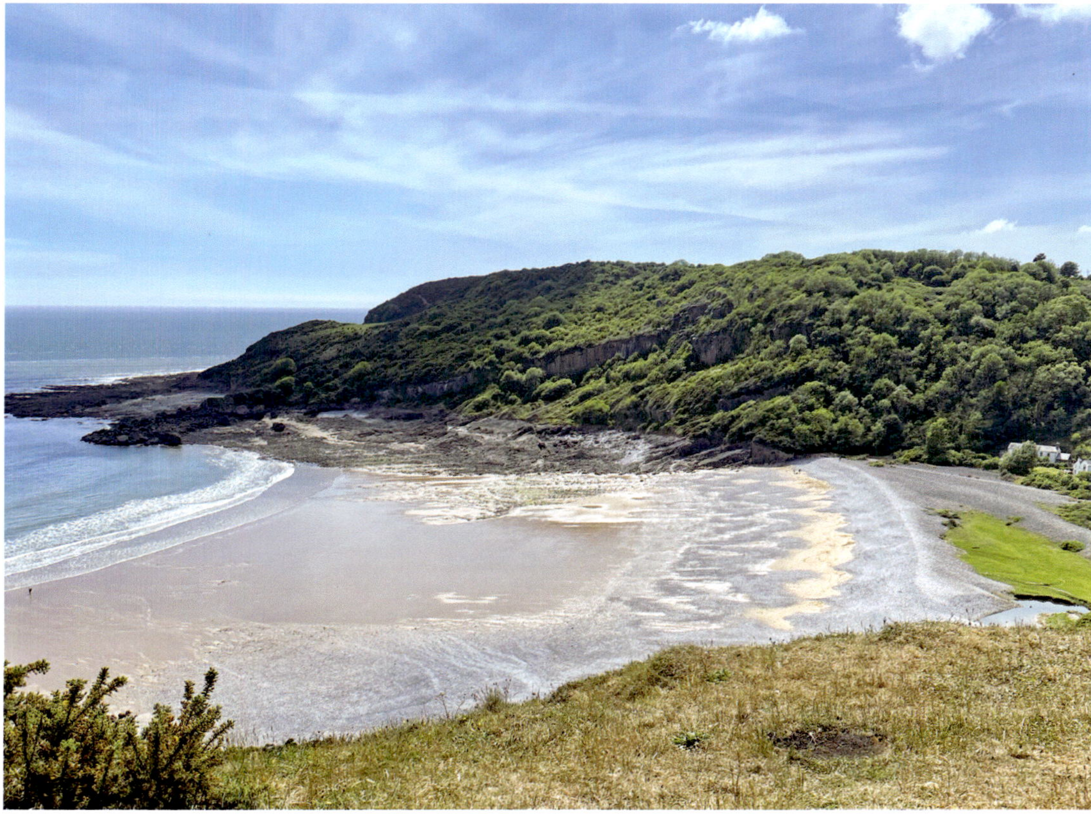

Pwlldu Bay. (© Alan Hughes, CC BY-SA 2.0)

Cultural Curiosities

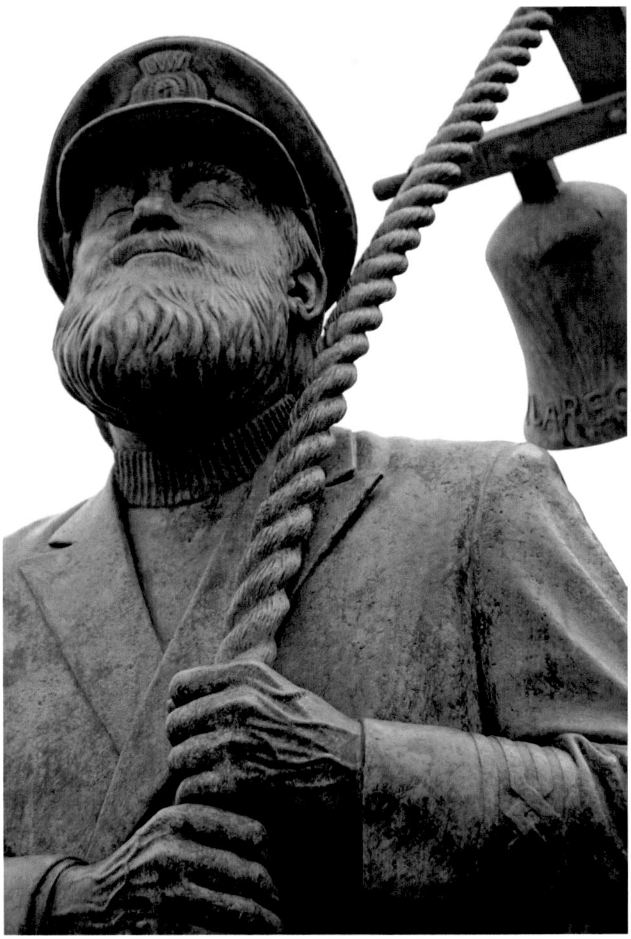

Captain Cat from Dylan Thomas's *Under Milk Wood* overlooking Swansea Marina. (© Chris Jobling, Flickr, CC BY-SA 2.0)

As we have seen in this book, in days gone by, the supernatural were naturally drawn to historical places with links to the distant past. A crumbling Gothic castle or a windswept cove made the perfect home for any self-respecting spook, but in more recent centuries, they have grown increasingly inseparable from our places of leisure. There's barely a town in Britain without a haunted theatre, museum, or pub, and in this final chapter we look at some of Swansea's cultural destinations where a quick pint or a night at the opera might get a little spookier than expected.

Swansea Grand Theatre

Like all good Victorian theatres of a certain vintage, Swansea Grand Theatre has had many a ghost sighting during its illustrious history. The city's flagship theatre first opened in 1897 and, despite much renovation, retains many of its original features and, it would appear, its resident phantoms. The most regularly sighted is the so-called woman in white, who reached the peak of her popularity in the 1980s when a storm of media attention resulted in a national TV breakfast programme conducting a séance at the theatre.

There are many theories as to the identity of the woman in white, with a popular suggestion being Adelina Patti, the superstar soprano who officially opened the theatre in the late nineteenth century. A woman matching her description dressed in Victorian or Edwardian clothing has been spotted in one of the boxes overlooking the stage, and she is accompanied by the scent of violets, her favourite flowers. Patti, however, is also said to haunt several other places with arguably a greater personal connection, such as the Patti Pavilion on Mumbles Road, her beloved winter garden that she donated to the city, and Craig-y-Nos Castle, her majestic mansion in the Swansea Valley.

Another potential suspect was Jenny Lind, the singer dubbed the 'Swedish Nightingale' who, it is claimed, performed at the Grand in 1912 before setting off across the Atlantic on the ill-fated *Titanic*. This was a nice theory until Ian Parsons, in his extensive history of the theatre, identified a problem: Lind died in Worcestershire in 1887, a decade before the theatre opened its doors. An alternative version of this story swaps Lind for a nameless woman working in the wardrobe department who fell in love with an American actor and was on her way to join him. Does she now haunt the last place they were happy together?

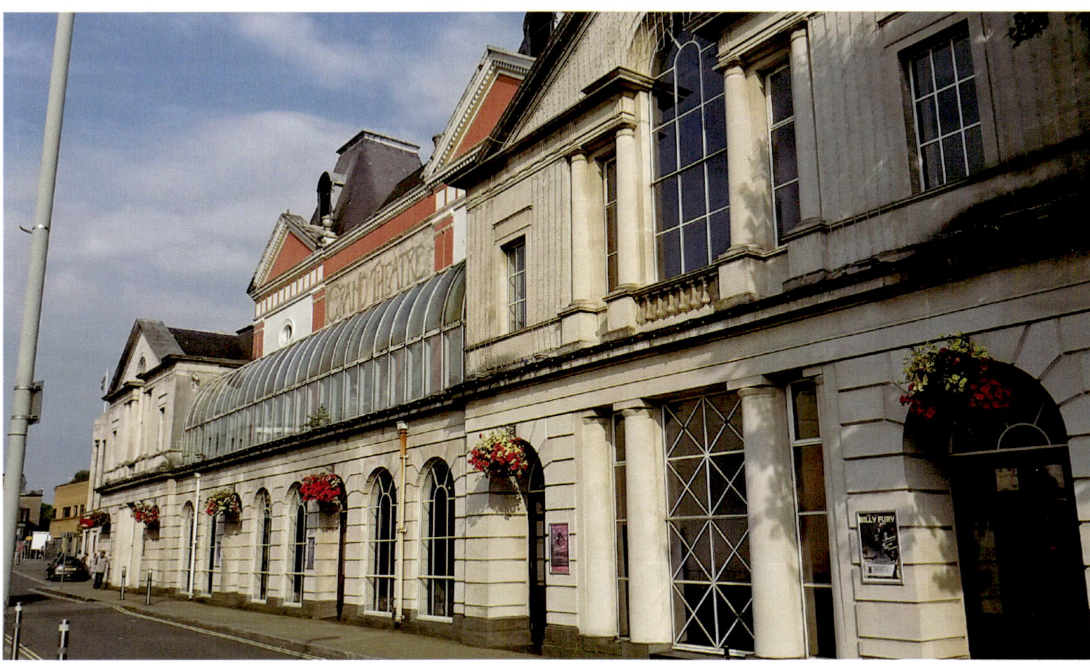

Swansea Grand Theatre.

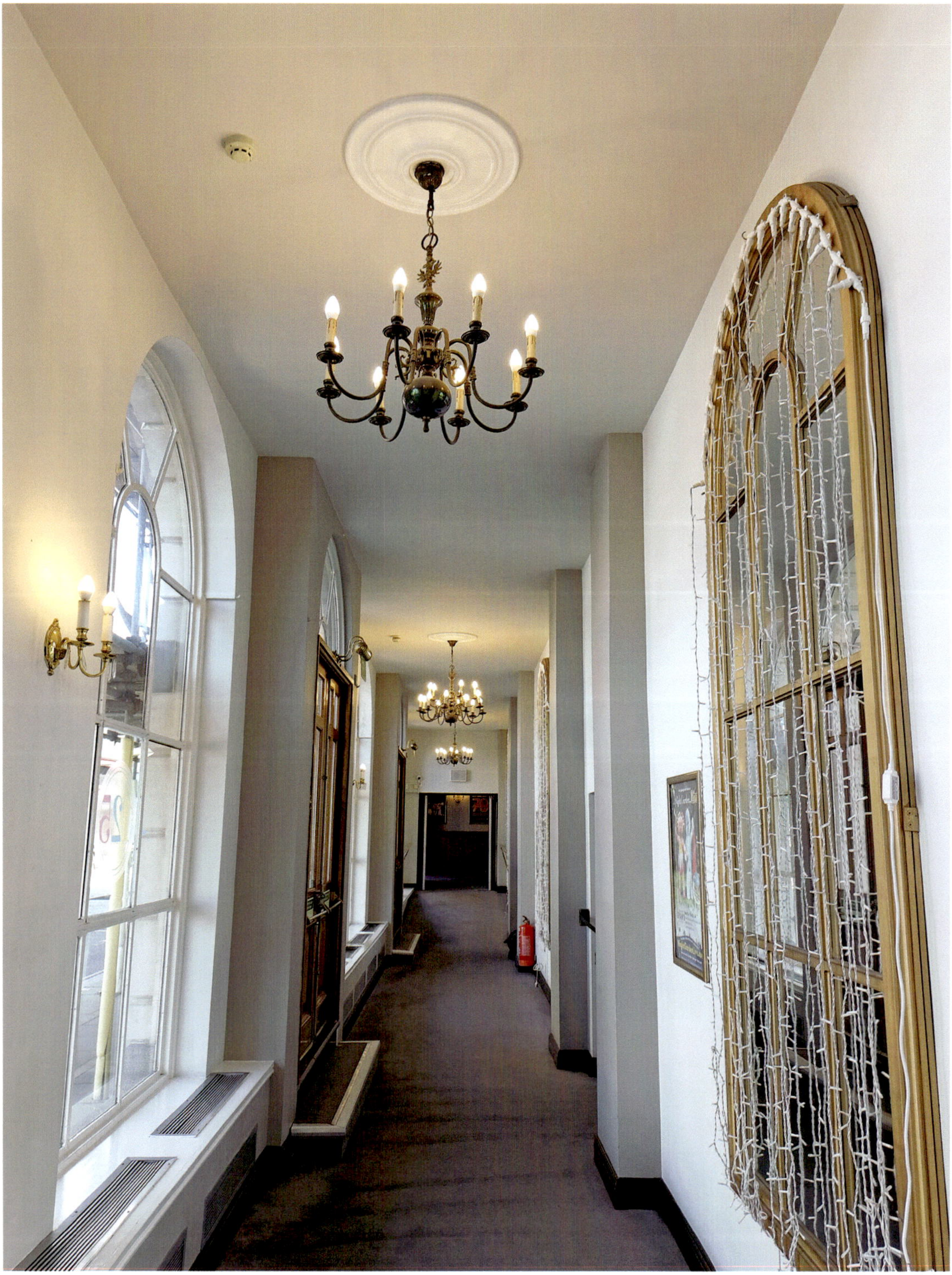

Inside Swansea Grand Theatre. (Katrina Merrell)

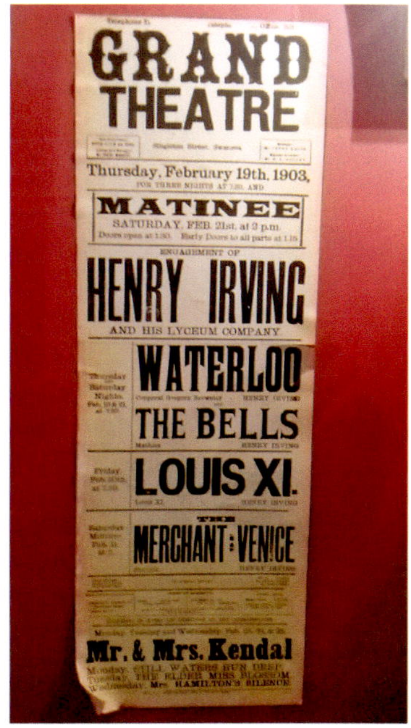

A poster for Henry Irving's show in 1903.

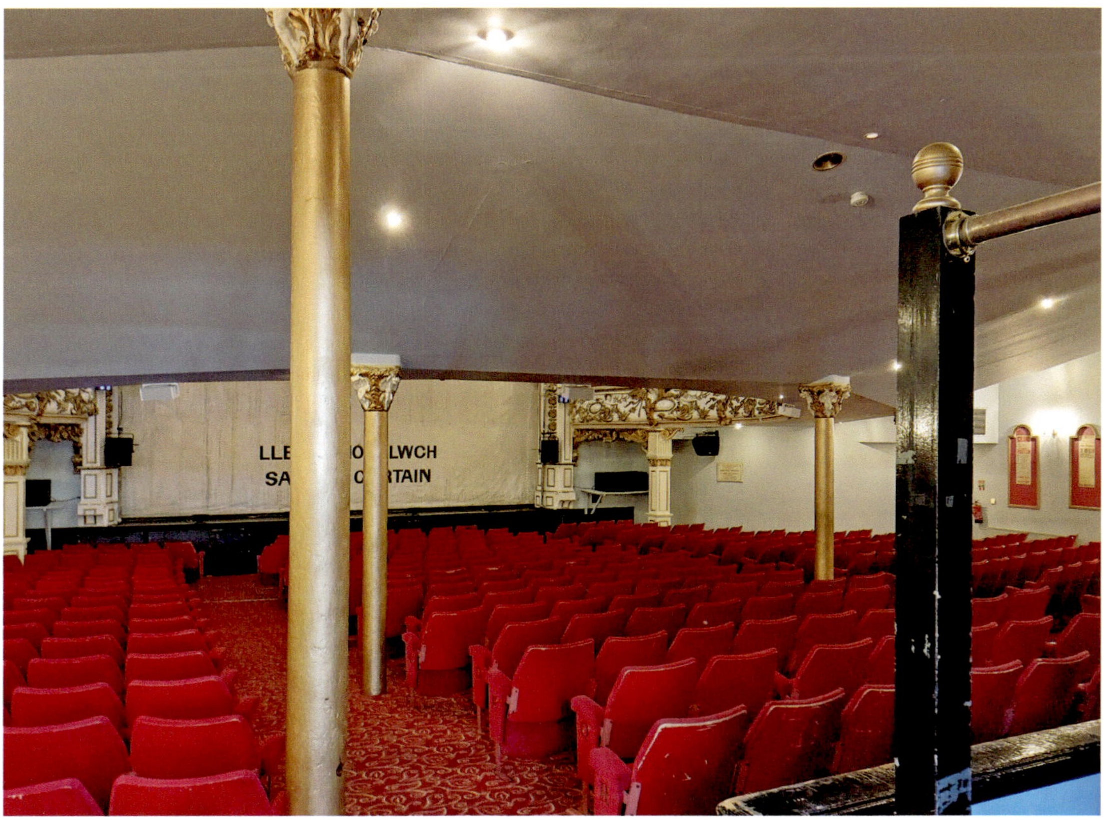

Downstairs in the auditorium at Swansea Grand Theatre. (Katrina Merrell)

The final theory also involves a tragedy at sea, and even has an uncanny connection to the most famous vampire of all. The theatre opened in the same year that Bram Stoker published *Dracula*, who visited Swansea soon after in his role as manager of Sir Henry Irving, the celebrated Shakespearean actor believed to have inspired the blood-sucking count. Irving appeared on stage many times in the city, sometimes alongside his daughter-in-law, the Swansea-born performer Mabel Lucy Hackney Irving, who married his son Laurence in 1903. They performed in her hometown annually from 1911 until 1913 and were due to return in 1914 when both she and her husband were killed in the RMS *Empress of Ireland* disaster. On her final visit to the theatre, she is said to have promised her wardrobe assistant that she would return the following year. The night she died, and before the news broke in the press, she appeared briefly in front of her dresser and spoke to her startled assistant, saying: 'I told you I would return, but I can't really stay long.'

One soprano who has had her own spooky experiences at the theatre as both a performer and a punter is Bronwen Beckett. In 2000, she was starring in Swansea Amateur Operatic Society's production of *Calamity Jane*, and while backstage in one of the dressing rooms with a fellow performer she was looking at photographs on the table when she felt someone creep up behind her and place a hand on her left shoulder. She recalls: 'I thought that another performer had come into the room without us noticing as we were so wrapped up in the photos and I turned but there was no one there. Puzzled, I turned back to my friend thinking he must have been playing a trick on me, but I could see both his arms on the table. The touch was not at all frightening. In fact, it felt incredibly comforting.' On the other side of the curtain, Beckett recalls watching a 'pretty awful' matinee in the circle when she felt 'almost icy fingers stroking my head'. She looked around and there was nobody nearby who could have touched her, but again she found the experience to be more comforting than frightening, 'as if they were agreeing with my thoughts on the performance'. On another occasion she was sitting at the back of the stalls with a friend watching medium Derek Acorah when they both felt a 'strong icy blast of air' as if someone had opened the door. At the same time, Acorah was drawn from the stage to speak to the person behind them. They assumed it was a coincidence, but when she told the story to a producer working at the theatre some time afterwards, he revealed he also had a 'ghostly encounter in exactly the same place'. He was sitting with a colleague in an otherwise empty auditorium watching a dress rehearsal when something made them turn around. They watched in awe as the seats in the row behind them moved in such a way that suggested someone was walking along the row. As a performer, Beckett has a unique insight into the world of theatre and has her own thoughts on what might be happening: 'I can understand why many theatres are haunted. So much emotional energy goes into every performance that all this energy must imprint itself on the fabric of the building. Performers who make the audience laugh and cry, putting their heart and soul into every performance – just think about all that emotional energy. What happens to it? Does it dissipate immediately after the curtain falls? Or does some of it linger?'

Former manager Vivyan Ellacott, meanwhile, recalled how in 1968 he and stage manager Philip Ormond were working late during a particularly stormy night. At 2 a.m. they noticed a single gas light was still on in the dress circle, and as he climbed the stairs to extinguish it Ormond joked that he should watch the ghost doesn't get him. As he reached out to turn the light off he saw the switch move by itself, felt a presence behind him, and smelt the distinctive smell of lavender. He dashed downstairs and outside to the safety of the car where Philip confessed that he had seen something for the briefest of moments standing behind his friend. A few years later, Eleanor Thomas was performing in *A Streetcar Named Desire* when she was amazed to see a woman in the circle emanating a dazzling white light. When she told Ellacott about it he could surely relate to the experience.

Swansea Museum

Don't let Swansea Museum's sophisticated façade and Greek columns fool you. Inspired by Egyptian architecture, the popular tourist attraction is home to a mummy who lived in Egypt between 250–200 BC, and more recently gave shelter to Swansea's most diabolical resident, a 3-foot-tall 'cursed' sculpture which, according to legend, is responsible for destroying a church. Unexplainable sounds, creeping shadows and chilling cold spots have been reported inside, and one long-serving member of staff has had first-hand experience of paranormal investigating there after dark. They personally witnessed a glass moving around a table by itself during a séance in the basement, and report that investigators have recorded inexplicable voices, witnessed the pages of the broadsheet *Cambrian* newspaper seemingly turning by themselves, and in the early 2000s a medium claimed that a man called George was wandering around upstairs looking for his coin collection.

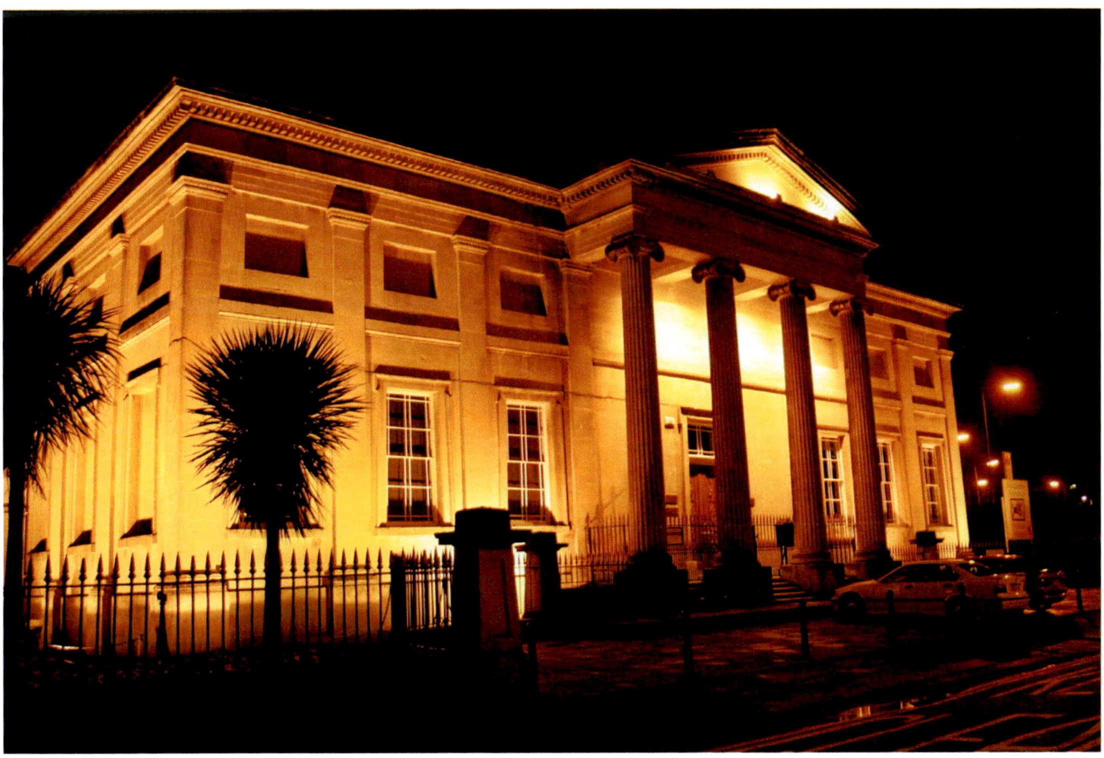

Swansea Museum by night. (© Swansea Museum/Swansea Council)

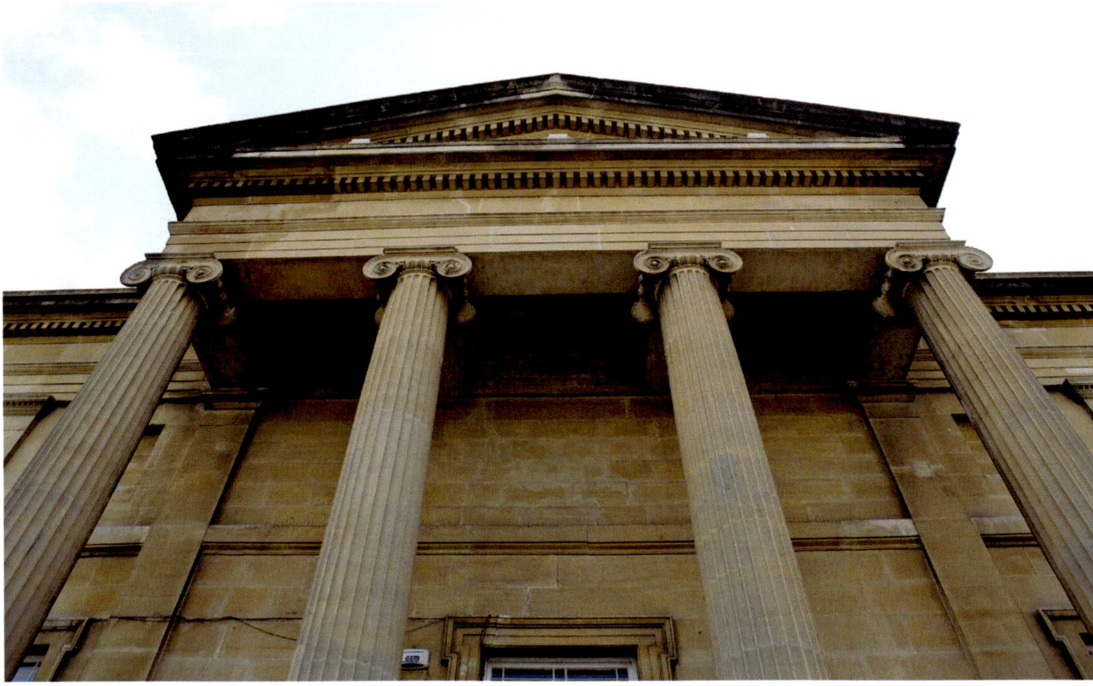

Swansea Museum's grand façade. (© Swansea Museum/Swansea Council)

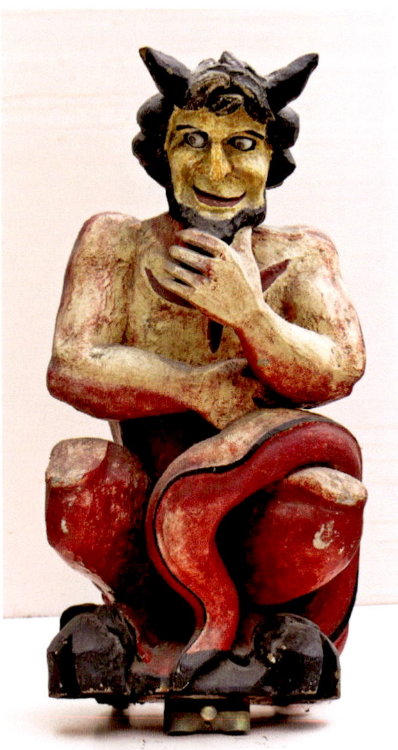

The Swansea Devil. (© SWWMedia)

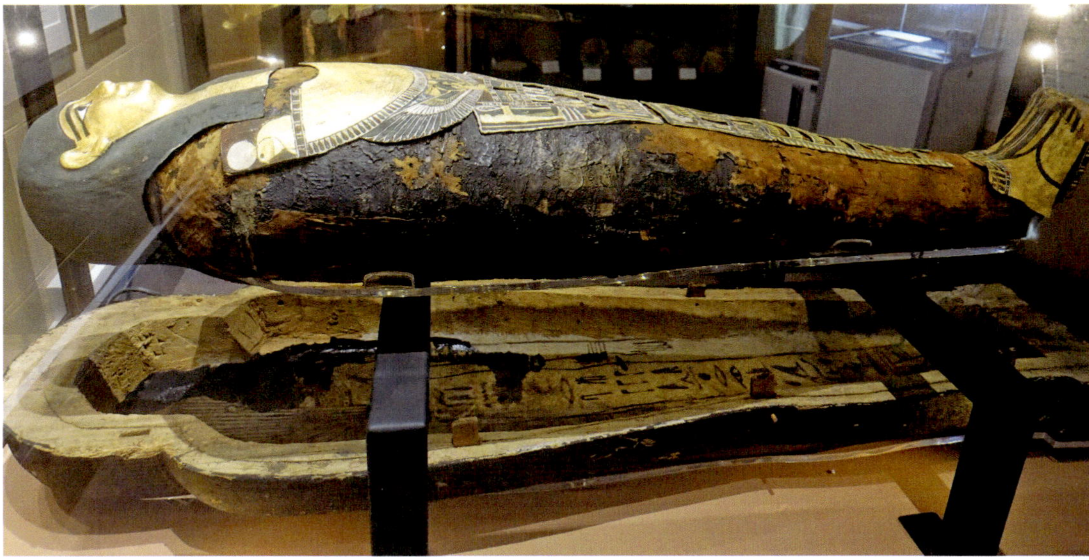

Egyptian Mummy at Swansea Museum. (© Tiia Monto, CC BY-SA 3.0)

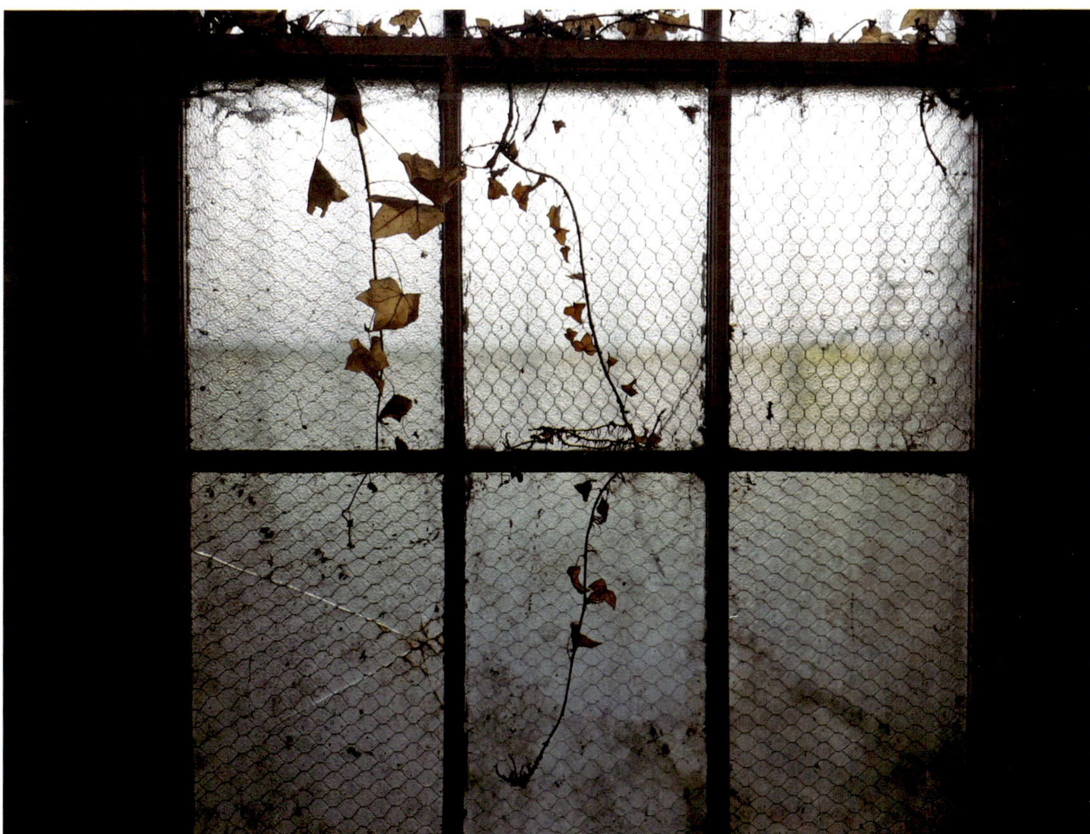

A basement window in Swansea Museum.

The story of the Swansea Devil begins in the late nineteenth century when architects were invited to submit their designs for St Mary's Church in the centre of town. The contract was awarded to Sir Arthur Blomfield, a prominent English architect whose completed church was met with almost universal acclaim when it was revealed in 1896. According to legend, however, one local architect seethed with jealousy at the injustice he saw in the contract being awarded to a famous outsider and vowed revenge. He snapped up the land next to the church and created his own buildings on which he placed a statue of 'Old Nick' staring directly at that hated church. He prophesied that: 'My devil will be able to leer and laugh, for at some future time he will see St Mary's burning to the ground.' That's exactly what happened during the Second World War. In 1941, much of Swansea city centre was destroyed during a ferocious Luftwaffe bombing campaign known as the 'Three Days' Blitz', and as the church burned, the Swansea Devil, safely perched on one of the few buildings to survive, watched on.

The Swansea Devil remained in place until 1962 when the offices were demolished, after which he vanished without a trace. He was tracked down in the 1980s by historian Rowley Davies and the *South Wales Evening Post* who discovered that he was gathering dust in an antique dealer's garage in Hereford. He was collected and returned by journalist Chris Peregrine and photographer Alan Trethewy, and it was decided that his new home should be the Quadrant Shopping Centre, next door to his old nemesis the church. He rarely stayed in the same place for long inside the Quadrant and spent time overlooking the entrance and guarding the market until it was decided that the statue, showing signs of age, would be better cared for by the experts at the museum. In 2019 the Swansea Devil went on permanent display, safely sealed in a glass cabinet that the curators have carefully positioned so that he still stares in the direction of St Mary's.

Wind Street and Swansea Castle

Swansea Castle is easily the city's most visible castle, if for no other reason than its prominent location bang in the middle of town. Sadly, when it comes to ghost stories it keeps its secrets closely guarded, and even those we do know of are frustratingly lacking in detail. Standing at the top of Wind Street, Swansea's party capital where countless spirits of a different kind are consumed, its position near the River Tawe was originally chosen for strategic reasons in the twelfth century. The ruins date from the thirteenth and fourteenth centuries and legend speaks of an underwater tunnel that links it with Oystermouth Castle, home of the White Lady in Mumbles. In more recent times it has played a key role in Swansea life as the site of a market, prison, town hall, and even the local newspaper office. The *South Wales Evening Post* later relocated to a multi-storey block in Adelaide Street where it remained for forty-five years, and where members of staff on the late shifts reported hearing movement on the deserted floors above and shadowy forms emerging from empty lifts.

Nowadays, Swansea Castle is not generally accessible to the public for safety reasons, but I was lucky enough to gain entry under supervision. My guide explained that those working behind the scenes have had several spooky experiences, although they were almost always fleeting, with the most common being shadowy shapes moving behind the windows on high, usually in the parapet. Most of the windows can be viewed from the street below and, as such, patient ghost hunters could observe

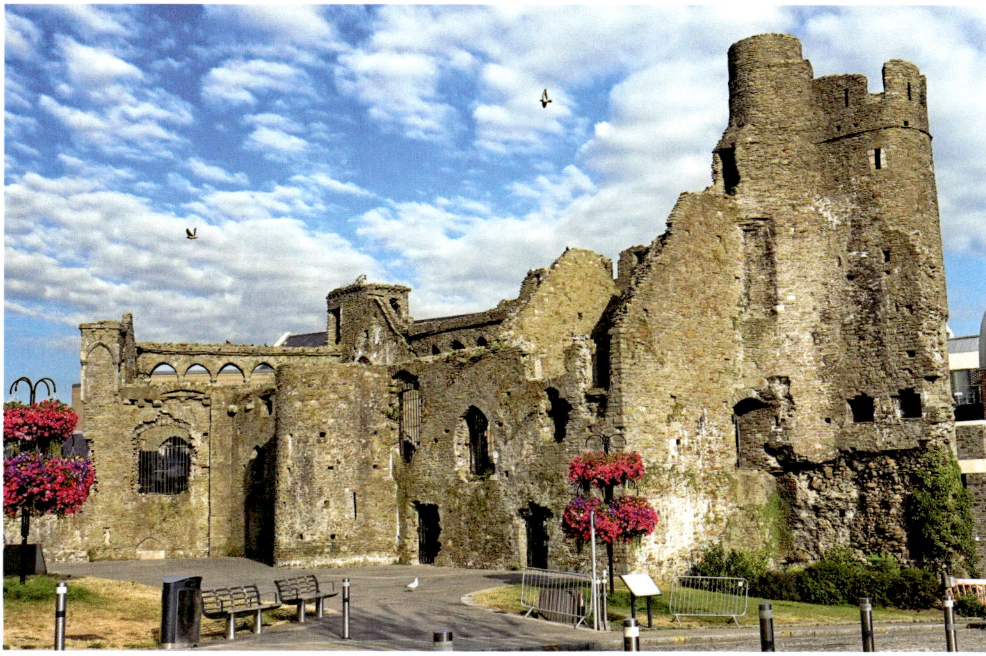

Swansea Castle. (© Tiia Monto, CC BY-SA 4.0)

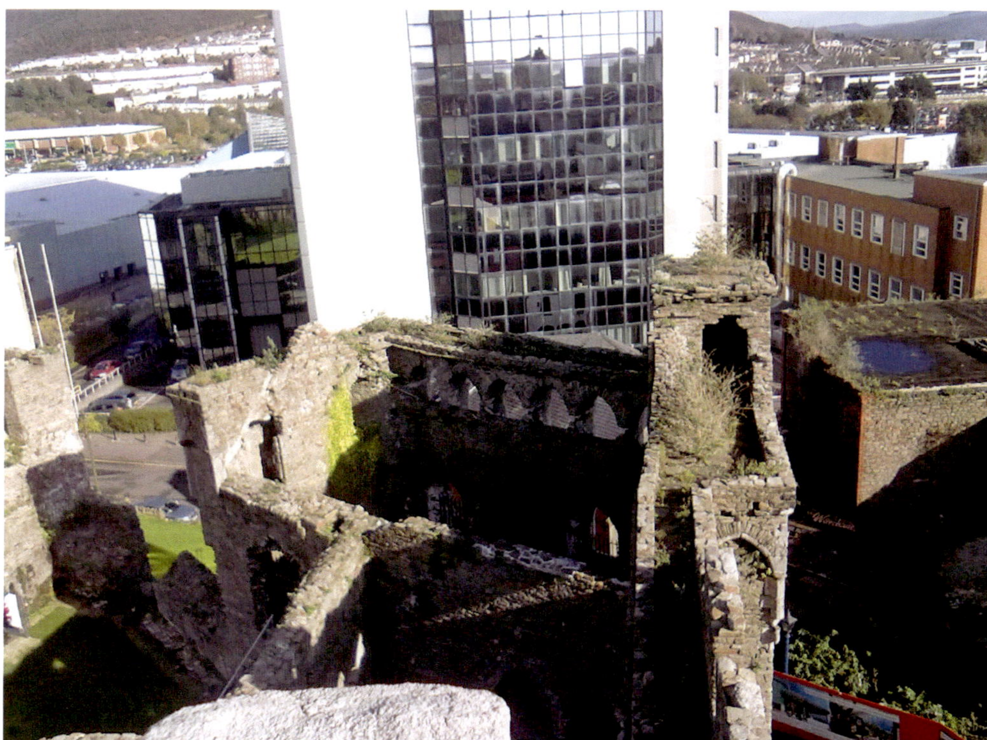

The view from the top of Swansea Castle.

them without needing access, although the constant hustle and bustle of city life makes it a difficult location for any serious investigation. The castle is also said to be haunted by a 'woman in blue' who disappears when approached, but beyond brief mentions in tourist literature, little is known about where this tale originated.

While not strictly paranormal, a pub that once stood on Wind Street a stone's throw from Swansea Castle has a tragic link with Gothic royalty. On 11 October 1816, there was a 'melancholy discovery' at the Mackworth Arms: the dead body of a young woman who had recently arrived from Bristol. She was found in her room with an empty bottle of laudanum and a suicide note. Her name was Fanny Imlay Godwin, the half-sister of *Frankenstein* creator Mary Shelley, whose husband Percy Bysshe Shelley was frantically dashing across the country in pursuit of his troubled sister-in-law. It is unknown if the Romantic poet made it to Swansea, but before Godwin's body was discovered, the name of the addressee on her suicide note had been torn off and burnt, suggesting that somebody had entered her room.

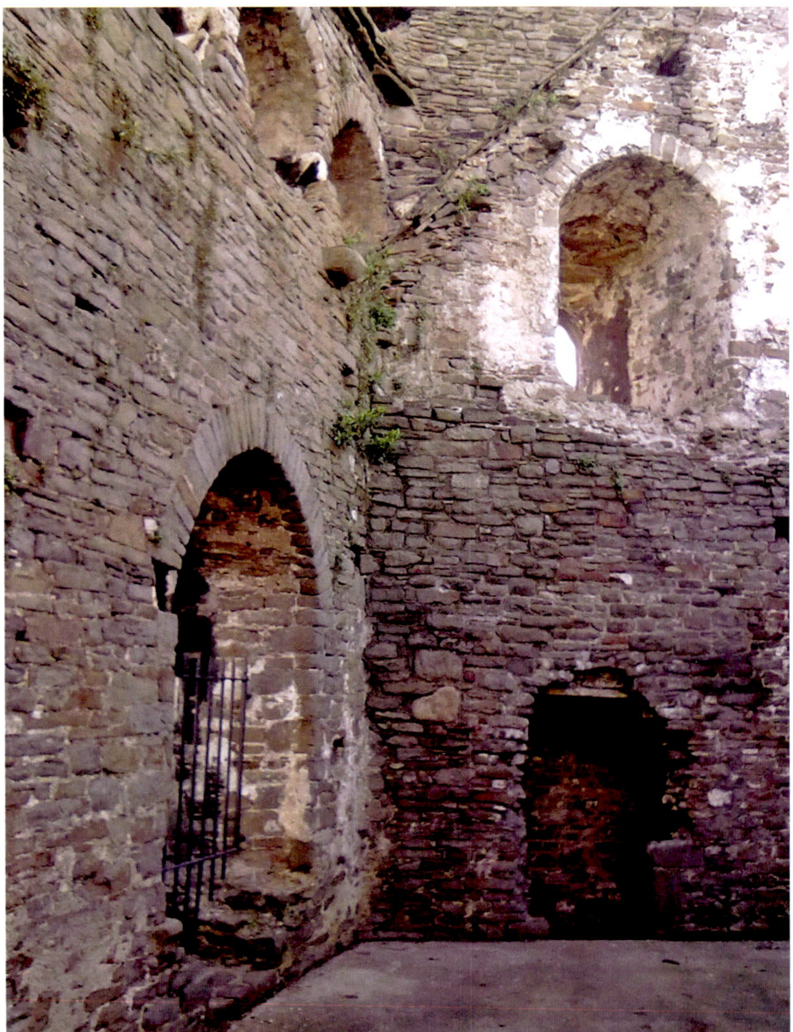

Exploring Swansea Castle.

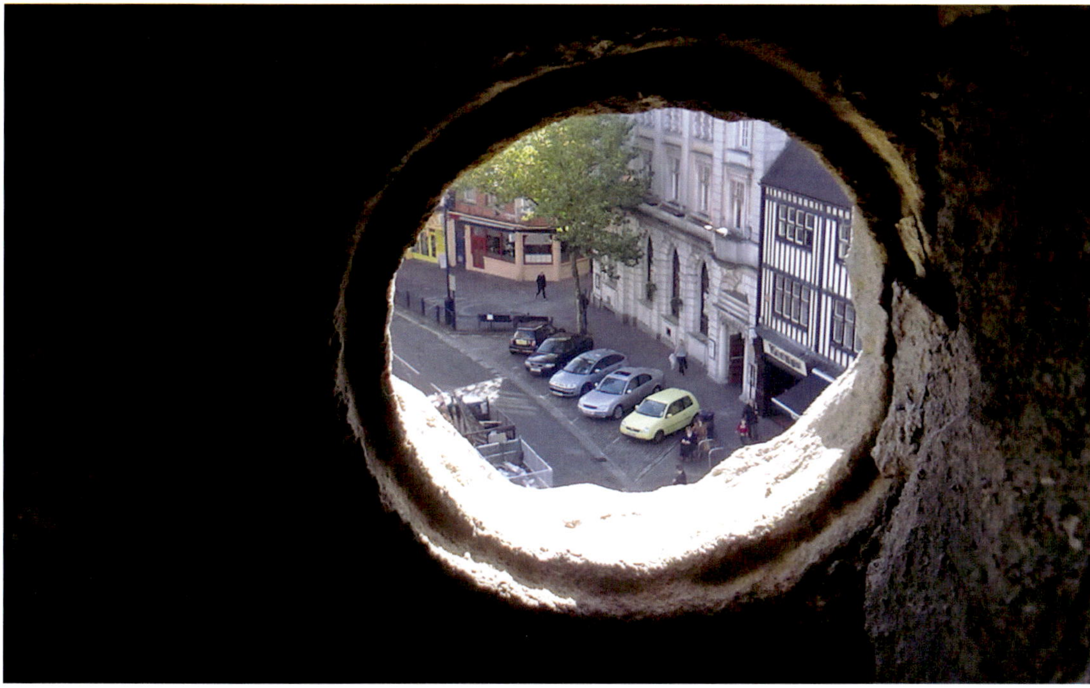

Looking down on Wind Street from Swansea Castle.

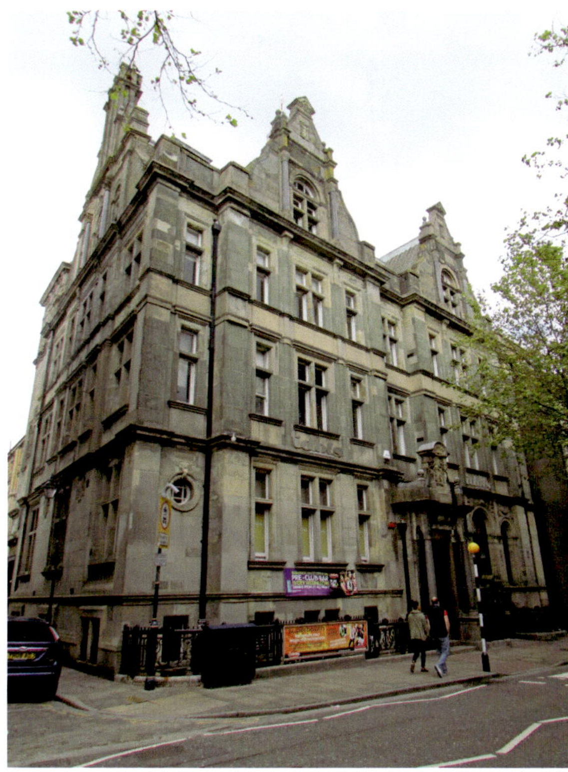

Wind Street. (© Tom Bastin, Flickr, CC BY 2.0)

1940s Swansea Bay

The 1940s Swansea Bay museum is home to a vast collection of objects either from or inspired by the Second World War. The ghosts said to be lurking within are also thought to date from the same period, which poses an interesting question: are they attracted there because of these items, or were they simply there anyway? In 2021, I joined Cymru Paranormal for an investigation, during which I spoke with owner John Thomas, who opened the attraction with his brother Huw in 2005. He explained that the museum was originally intended to span thousands of years of history, from the Vikings landing in Swansea to more recent times. If they'd stuck to their original vision, would that have changed the nature of the ghosts that now seemingly call it home?

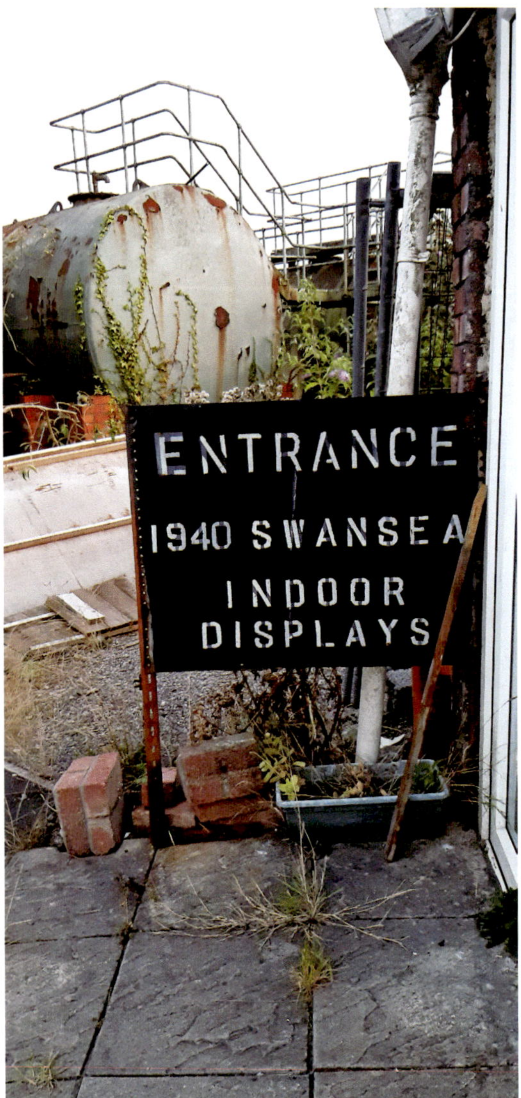

Welcome to 1940s Swansea Bay.

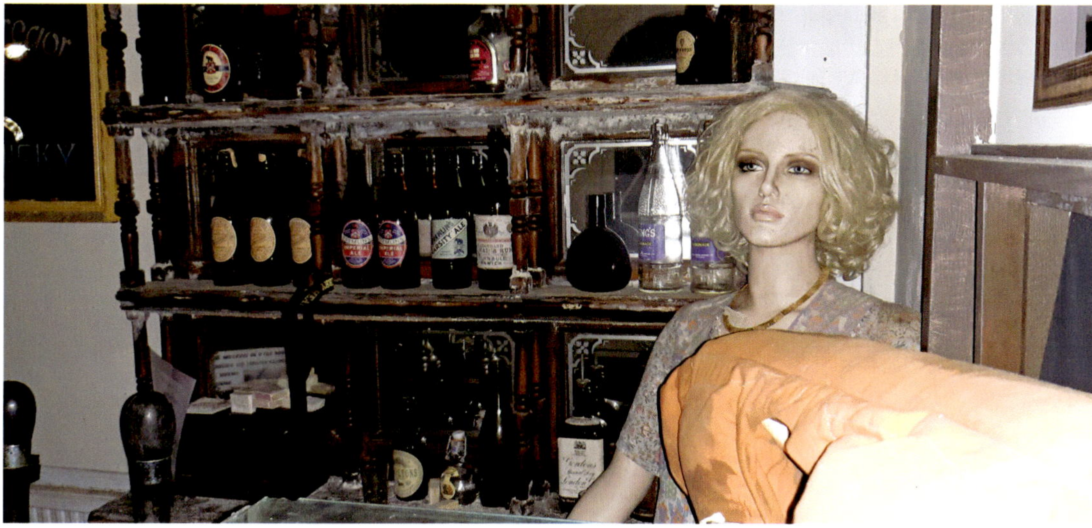

A mannequin behind the bar at 1940s Swansea Bay.

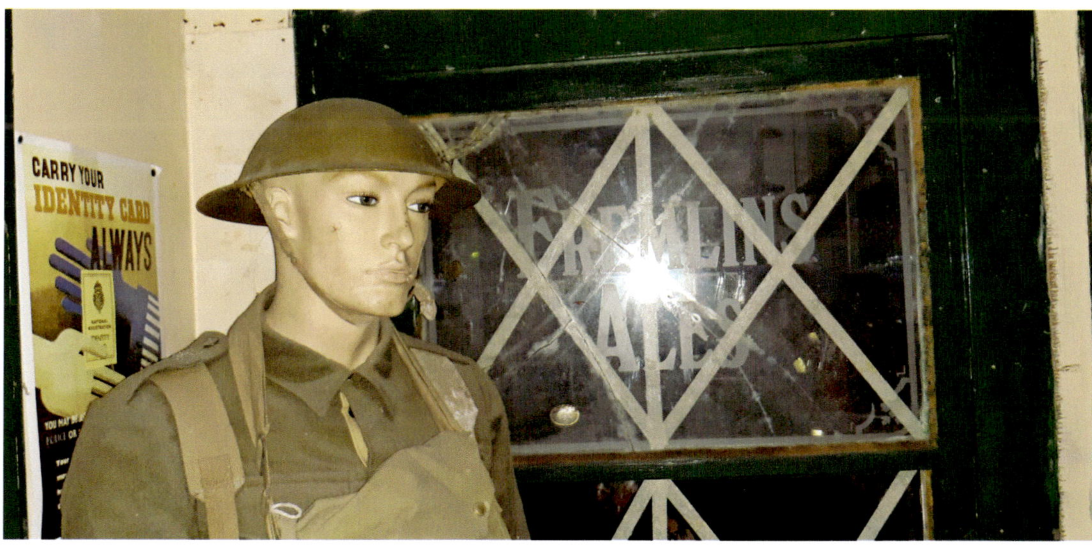

A soldier ready for battle at 1940s Swansea Bay.

The most common phenomena reported at the museum are moving shadows and the much-maligned orbs, which is hardly surprising in such a dusty old building. Reported sightings of ghostly figures include an RAF pilot and a man and woman who play cards in an area that has been recreated to look like a pub, although it should be noted that the museum is packed with mannequins dressed in period clothing. While these life-size models make it a wonderfully interactive learning experience for youngsters on a school trip, they can easily fool unsuspecting investigators once the lights go out – and I say that from experience! Ghost hunting groups have found that attempting to capture spectral voices on recording devices, known as electronic voice phenomenon (EVP), to be an effective method of communication. Some have even tried to provoke a reaction by playing pre-recorded music and voices from the 1940s, with a speech by Adolf Hitler said to have elicited a suitably angry response from a patriotic British serviceman whose hatred of the Führer had not diminished with time.

Spooky SA1

In the late 1990s, Swansea's SA1 area was reinvigorated with new offices, shops, and restaurants. The skyline-defining Millennium Bridge connected the docklands to the city centre, and businesses old and new flocked to this up-and-coming corner of town. One such company in search of a fixer-upper found what appeared to be the perfect property. It was in a sorry state and had possibly been used as a squat, but it was a bargain as a result and had lots of space for offices and parking. There was just one snag that they weren't aware of beforehand: it was supposedly haunted. What follows is an account of the haunting from a senior management figure who has asked to remain anonymous, and any personal details have been changed to protect the identity of those involved.

Following some structural work on the building, it began to fill with staff as the interior was still being finished. It was at this time that the manager had their 'first hint of anything uncomfortable' inside. One day they took their dog to the office, who was happily exploring somewhere new until they entered the manager's office. They remember that: 'It did not go well. She refused, point blank, to cross the threshold

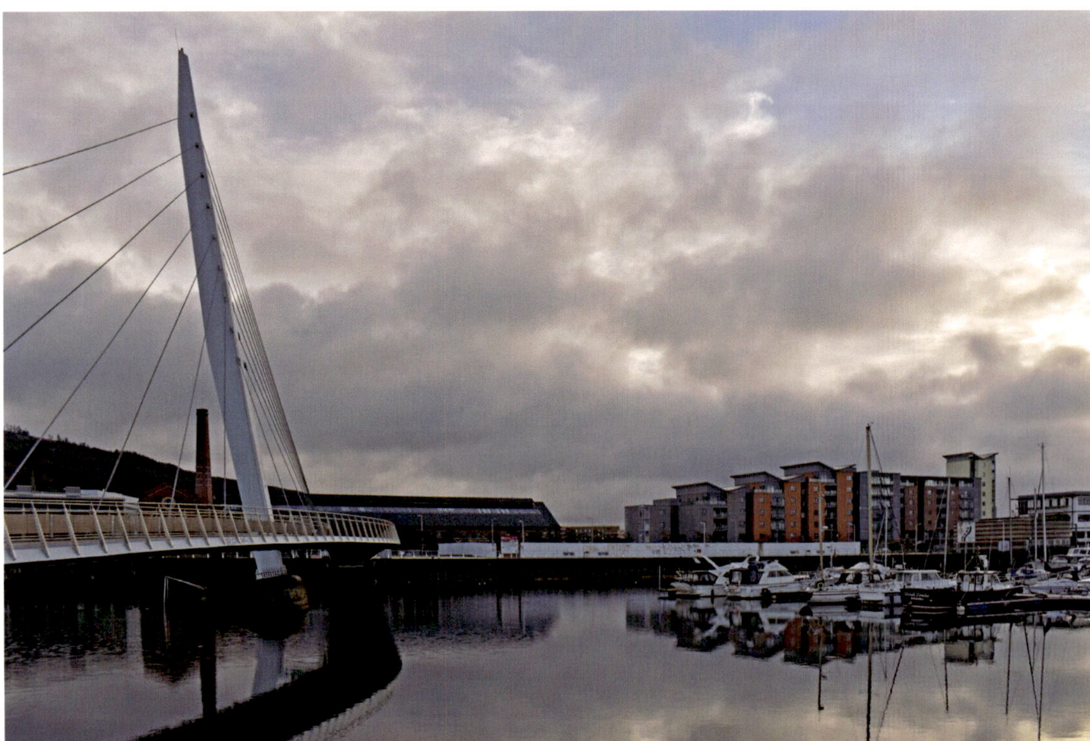

A view across Swansea's Millennium Bridge. (© Harshil Shah, Flickr, CC BY-ND 2.0)

into that room. I picked her up and carried her in. She was shaking in my arms and was looking for a way to leave. She resorted to cowering under my desk. She appeared completely terrified.' The manager was left with no choice but to take the dog home, but as soon as they walked out of the back door she was fine again.

On another occasion, an electrician was laying cables outside of office hours. He and a colleague were the only people in the building, which was securely locked and could only be accessed with a pass. As the sun set, they heard footsteps coming up the stairs from the ground floor. Assuming it must be somebody working late they thought nothing of it, but later realised that the stairs had been carpeted – how could they have heard feet on wood? Things got stranger when they saw a door open into a room on the floor below, and despite clearly hearing someone walking across the room towards a large window, there was nobody there. They looked at each other and made a sharp exit, finding the doors and gate securely locked as they fled. They refused to return, and contractors were hired to finish the job.

Another tradesperson to down tools following a strange experience was a decorator. They had been working in the building for weeks without incident, but that all changed one day as they sat on a stool painting a filing cabinet. They had their earphones in and were absorbed in their work when movement in the doorway caught their attention. It was a well-lit, well-ventilated room, and creeping towards them was something described as a dark mist that caused them to drop their paintbrush in fright. With the door being the only means of escape, they were forced to charge straight through whatever it might be, running down the stairs and into the manager's office. The manager recalls that 'whatever they had experienced really and truly had upset them'. Later that day they phoned to confirm that they would not be returning.

Despite experiencing nothing themselves at this point, the manager was aware of the staff's concerns about being in the building alone and increased security. The 'girls' often walked in pairs, and one morning, when they arrived to find the water had been cut off, they were too scared to go into the cellar to check the stop tap. When it was eventually investigated they discovered a major flood, but no explanation could be found as to how it started. On another occasion, the manager arrived early and as they picked up the mail from the floor heard a 'sustained metallic crashing sound' coming from the same cellar. It sounded like 'someone kicking a metal mop bucket around a room', and assuming it was an intruder they rushed back to their car and phoned the police and the operations manager. The latter was the first to arrive with three other men and, armed with torches, they headed into the cellar. They found it completely empty; no intruder, no metallic objects, nothing. The manager phoned the police back and could only apologise.

A possible explanation for the activity emerged when a member of staff who was not office based visited for a cup of tea. Out of the blue, they asked the manager if they knew the building was haunted, who laughed it off to avoid scaring the team. But the worker continued, explaining that they had a 'bit of a gift' and had seen a 'ghost' a few times at the bottom of the staircase, which had been the original entrance to the cellar before the renovation. They claimed it was a female ghost in an old-fashioned maid's outfit called Betsy who had been 'pushed down the cellar stairs to her death by a man who lived in the house'. The company has since relocated, but another intriguing piece of potential evidence emerged during the moving process. The manager was told by the estate agent that the building had a reputation for being haunted, and they believed there used to be a restaurant in the cellar with a haunted table. Had they been haunted by the same spirit that had haunted that table?

Welcome to Town

For more than three centuries, the Welcome to Town has been at the heart of village life in Llanrhidian. The historic inn has had many uses over the centuries, from a courtroom to a gaol to a masonic temple, some of which might explain the identities of its supposed resident ghosts. Now a popular food and drink establishment, perhaps the most oft-sighted supernatural visitor is believed to be a coachman named Henry who appears in Regency-era clothing either sitting at the bar or gazing out of the window, possibly at the mysterious stones that stand before Ss Rhidian and Illtyd. In more recent times, chef Steve Sawyer spoke about his own experiences to the local press: 'Sometimes when I go in at 7 a.m. on a Sunday I can hear footsteps from the floor above, which used to be a courtroom … There's also a corner that they say is home to a ghost and I have stood there and felt a presence.' Not that these experiences put him off his work in any way; in fact, it's just part of the job of working somewhere with such a rich history: 'It doesn't really scare me because I have worked in lots of pubs and most of them have a ghost of some kind.'

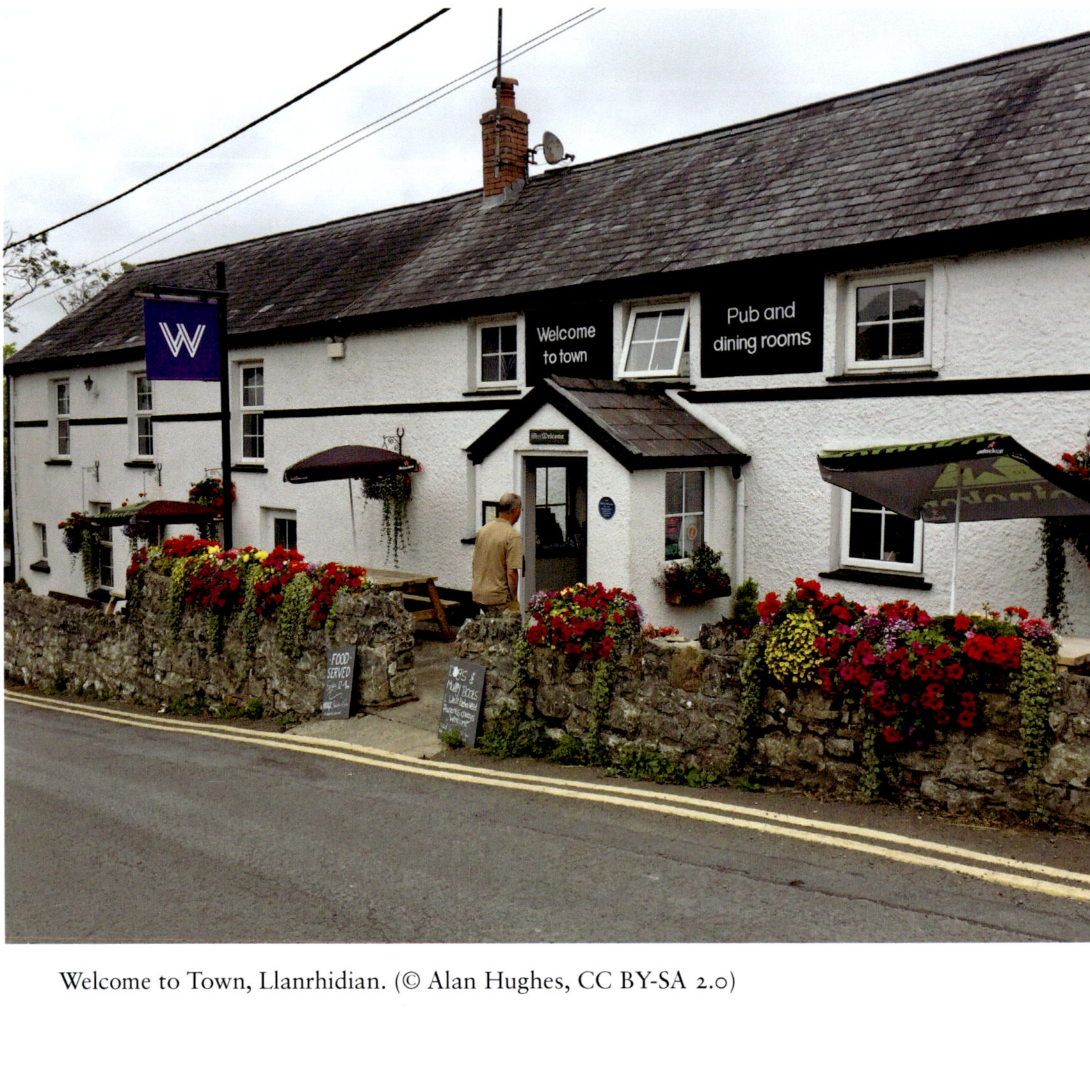

Welcome to Town, Llanrhidian. (© Alan Hughes, CC BY-SA 2.0)

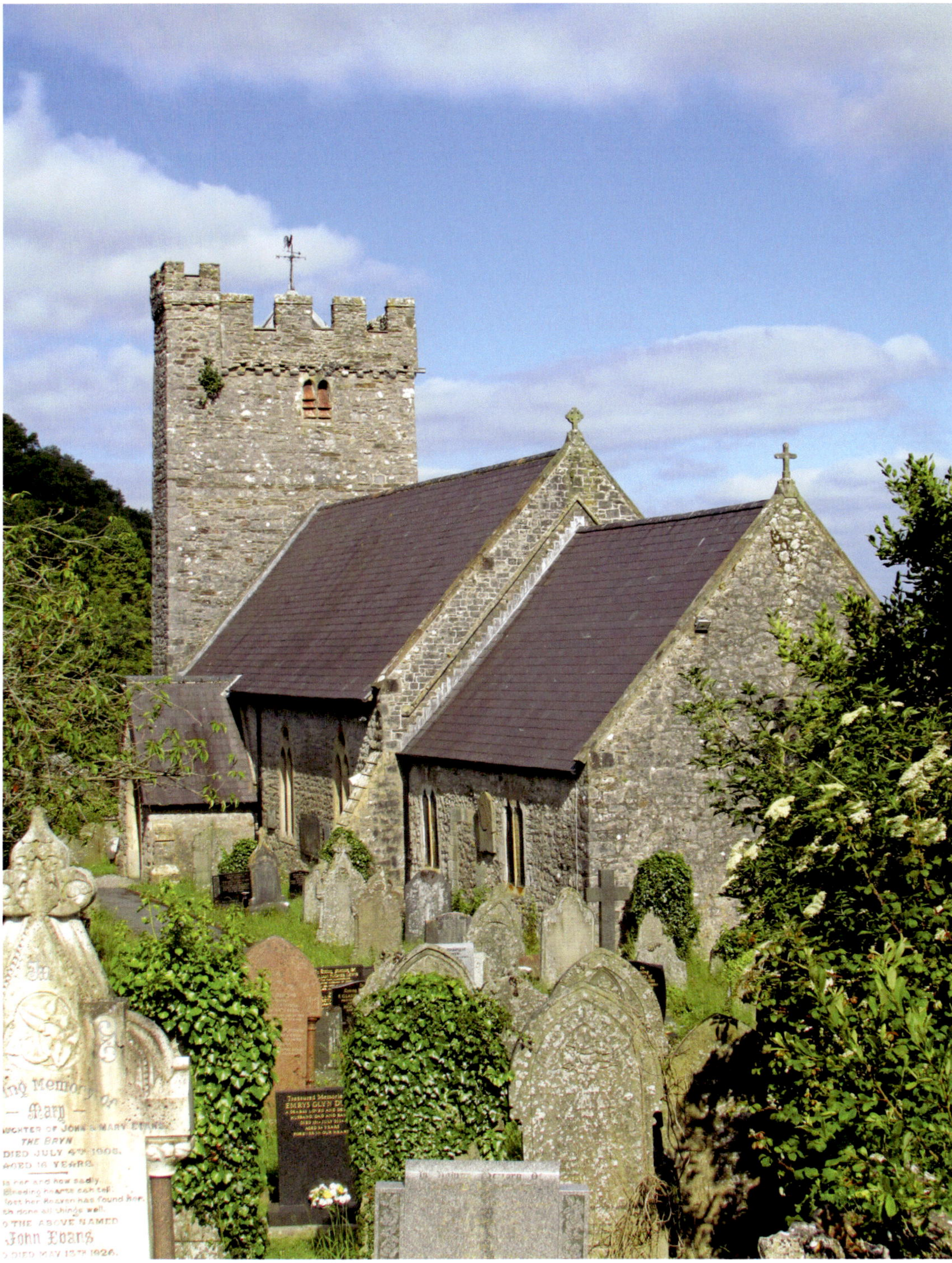

Ss Rhidian and Illtyd in Llanrhidian opposite the Welcome to Town. (© Tom Bastin, Flickr, CC BY 2.0)

Gower Heritage Centre

Gower Heritage Centre is a family-friendly museum with indoor and outdoor areas to explore. Built around a twelfth-century watermill, it stands on what was once a part of the Braose family estate, who established a vast deer park nearby. Having opened as a heritage attraction in 1989, it preserves the fascinating history of the peninsula and has become one of the best places in Wales to see the Mari Lwyd, a wassailing tradition in which a group of revellers parade a horse's skull around to welcome in the new year.

Much of the alleged paranormal activity appears to centre around the historical mill which has been heard turning on its own. Having spent a night or two there myself with groups of investigators, their equipment certainly suggested something in that area worthy of further investigation. They believed the main culprit for the disturbances was William Davies, more affectionately known as Will the Mill, a nineteenth-century worker whose family cared for the mill for five generations. A room adjacent to the mill has been recreated to resemble his cottage and is believed to be another ghostly hotspot, although Will, I am assured, is an entirely benign spirit who seems content to simply continue working in the afterlife.

In 2006, celebrity medium Derek Acorah filmed an episode of his *Ghost Towns* series in Swansea, the pinnacle of which was a visit to the centre. He was invited to investigate by resident artist Tony Paultyn who had noticed the figure of a man out of the corner of his eye while working in his watercolour studio, and invisible children who played with his train set. Acorah, who was joined by Myleene Klass and Rhodri Owen, seemed to confirm Paultyn's suspicions when he detected the 'energies' of around fifteen children. He also claimed they were being watched by two evil 'shapeshifters' who had tortured people in the past and were part of a dark conspiracy. Before leaving, he conducted a clearance to cleanse the building, and Tony said that he felt at peace afterwards.

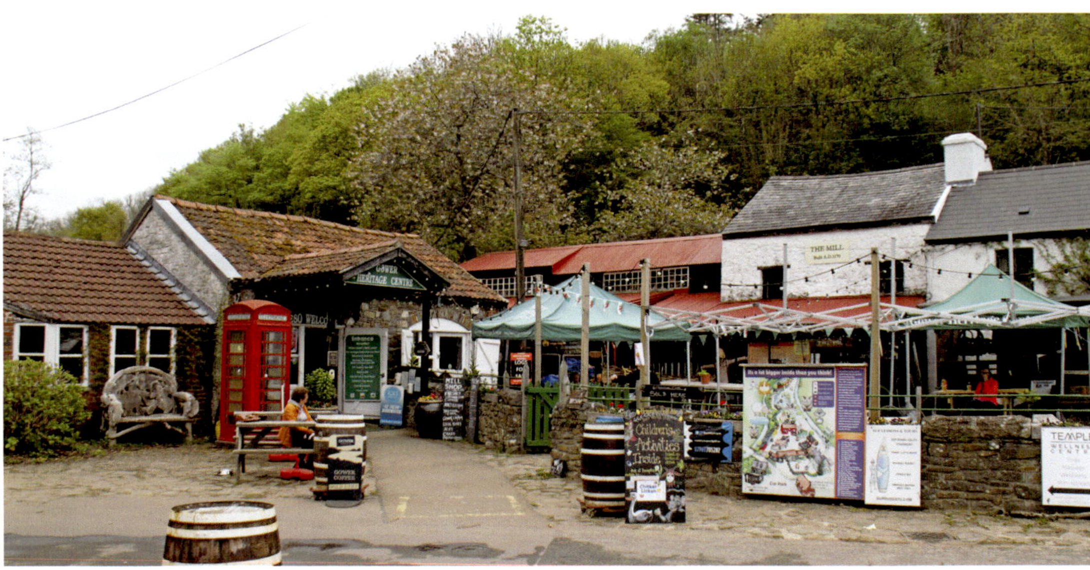

Gower Heritage Centre. (© Tony Hisgett, Flickr, CC BY 2.0)

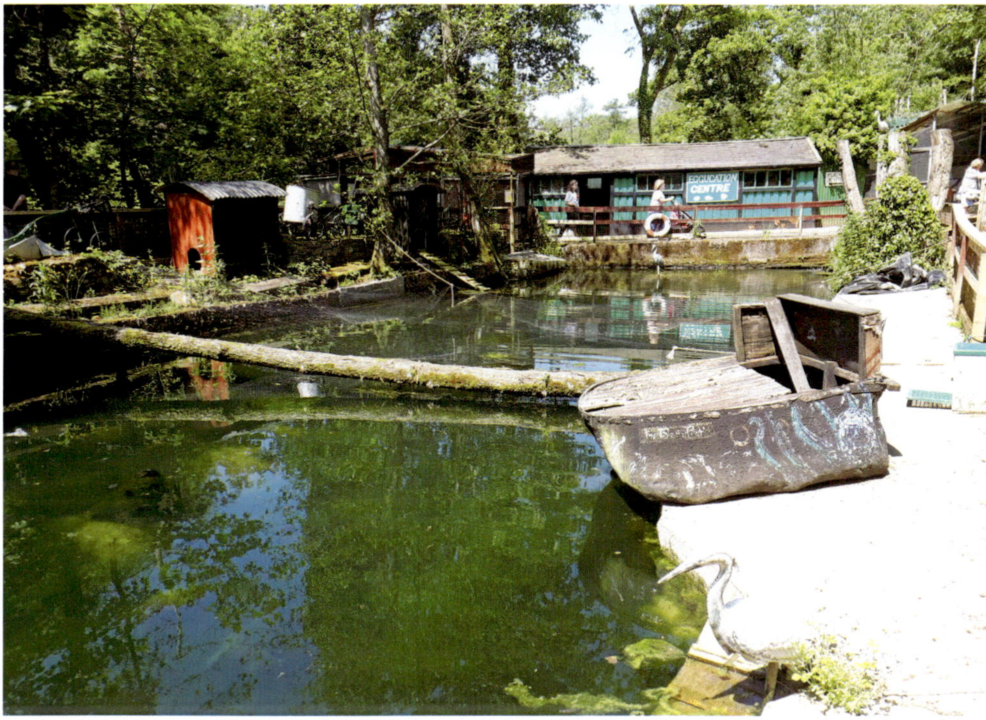

A coracle at the Gower Heritage Centre.

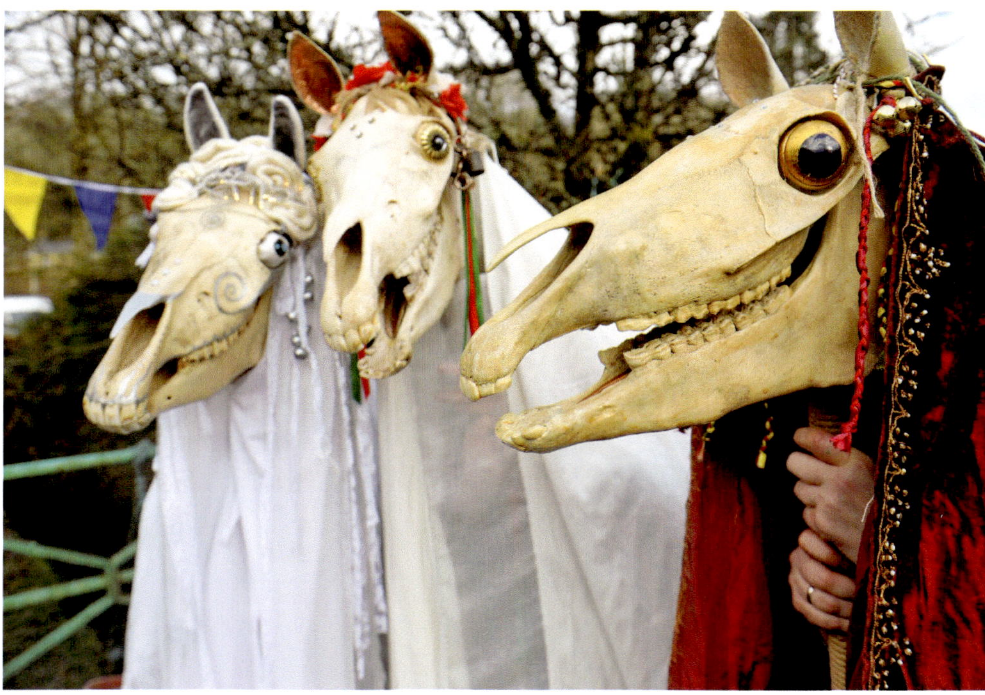

A trio of Mari Lwyds at the Gower Heritage Centre. (© SWWMedia)

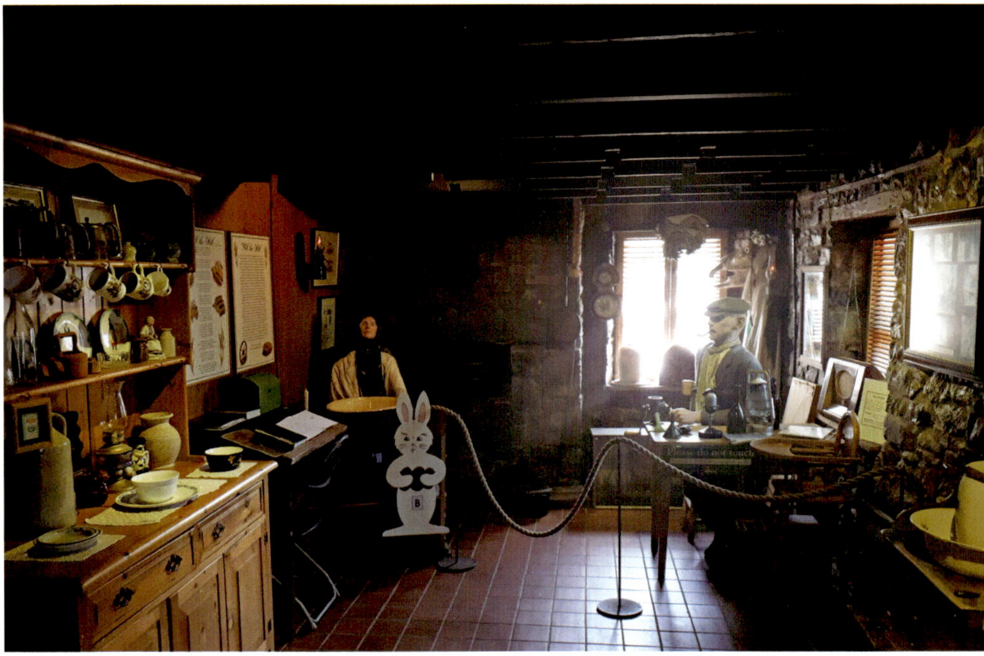

Inside Will the Mill's cottage at Gower Heritage Centre.

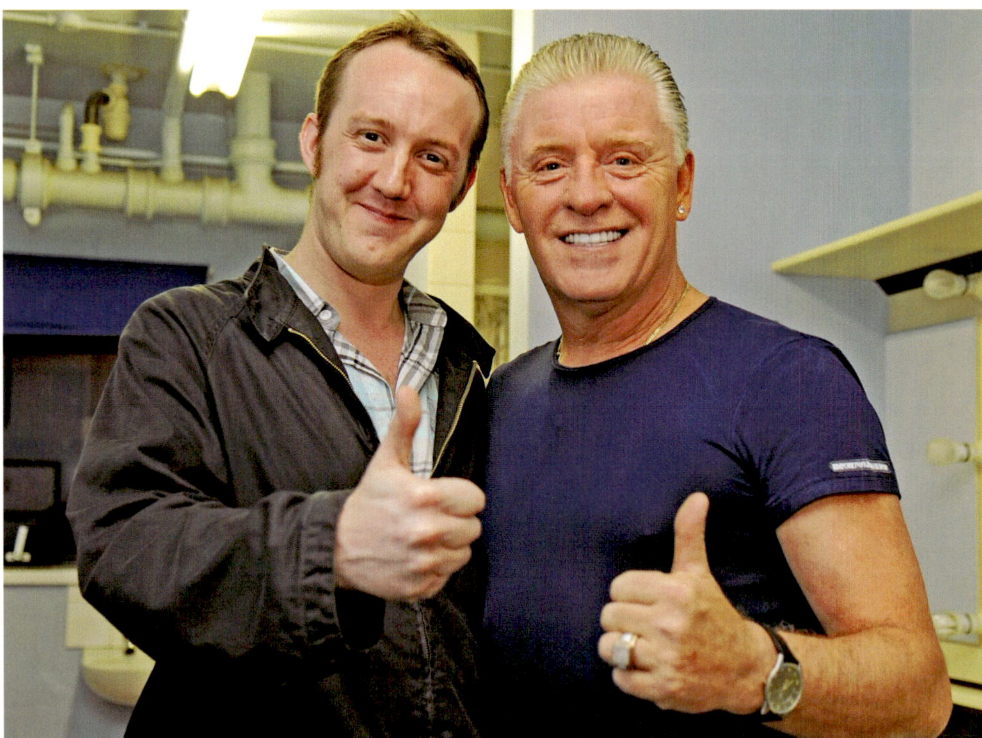

The author with Derek Acorah in Swansea in 2010. (Photo by Andrew Davies)

The Haunts of Dylan Thomas

The ghost of Dylan Thomas (1914–53) haunts Swansea in a figurative and, some would say, literal sense. He wrote widely of his formative years in the city, from the carol-singing sea to his favourite watering holes, and his words can be found dotted around the town today, from street art to sculptures. He also wrote the occasional ghost story, such as the eerie spinechiller *The Followers* (1952) in which two Swansea drinkers follow a woman home only to receive the fright of their lives. A statue of the man himself can be found overlooking the Marina, behind which is the Dylan Thomas Theatre, home to the long-running Swansea Little Theatre that Dylan was briefly a member of and where a 'presence' has been felt backstage. Just around the corner is the similarly named Dylan Thomas Centre which a former member of, and where staff claims is haunted by the figure of someone who died nearby before it opened its doors as an arts centre in 1995.

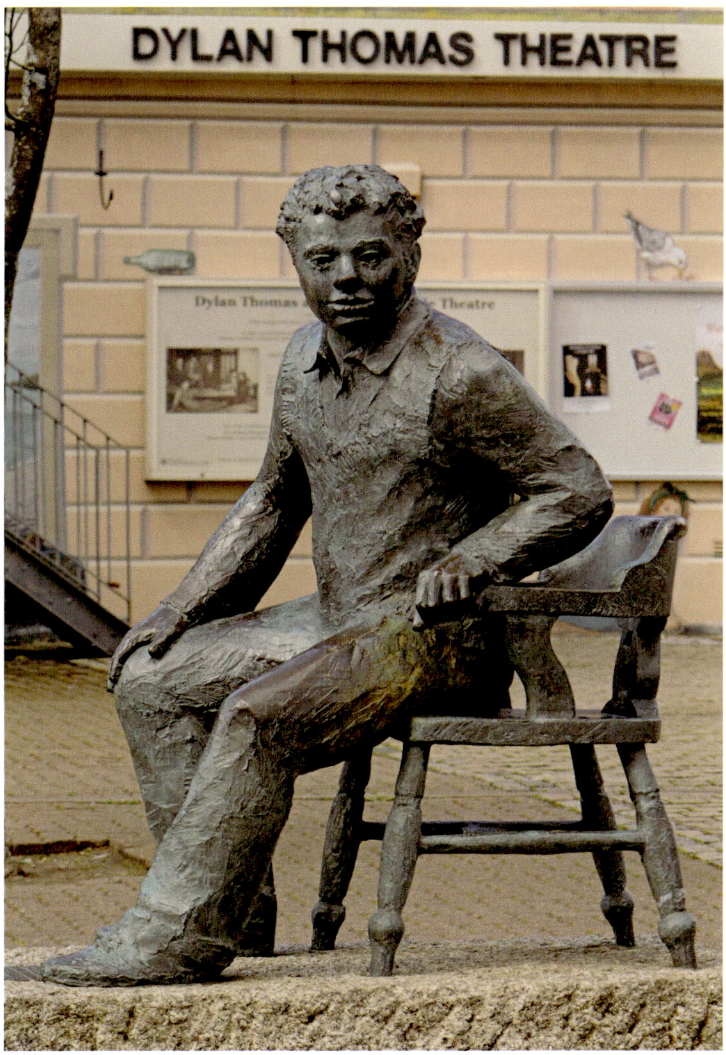

A statue of Dylan Thomas in Swansea Marina. (© Clint Budd, Flickr, CC BY 2.0)

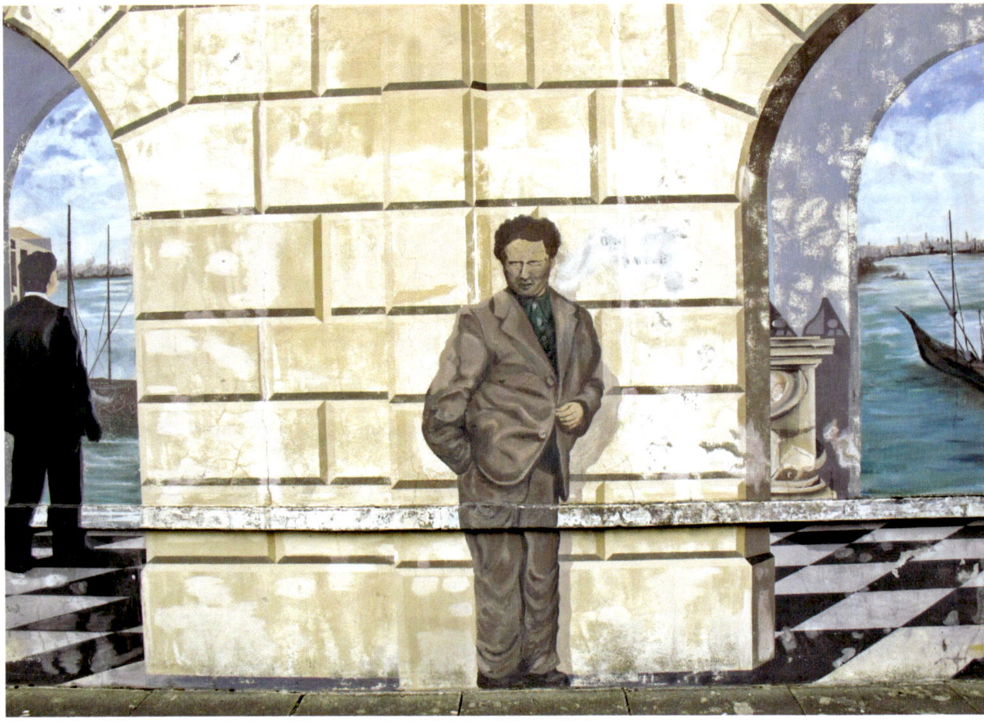

Dylan Thomas on the wall outside the Dylan Thomas Theatre.

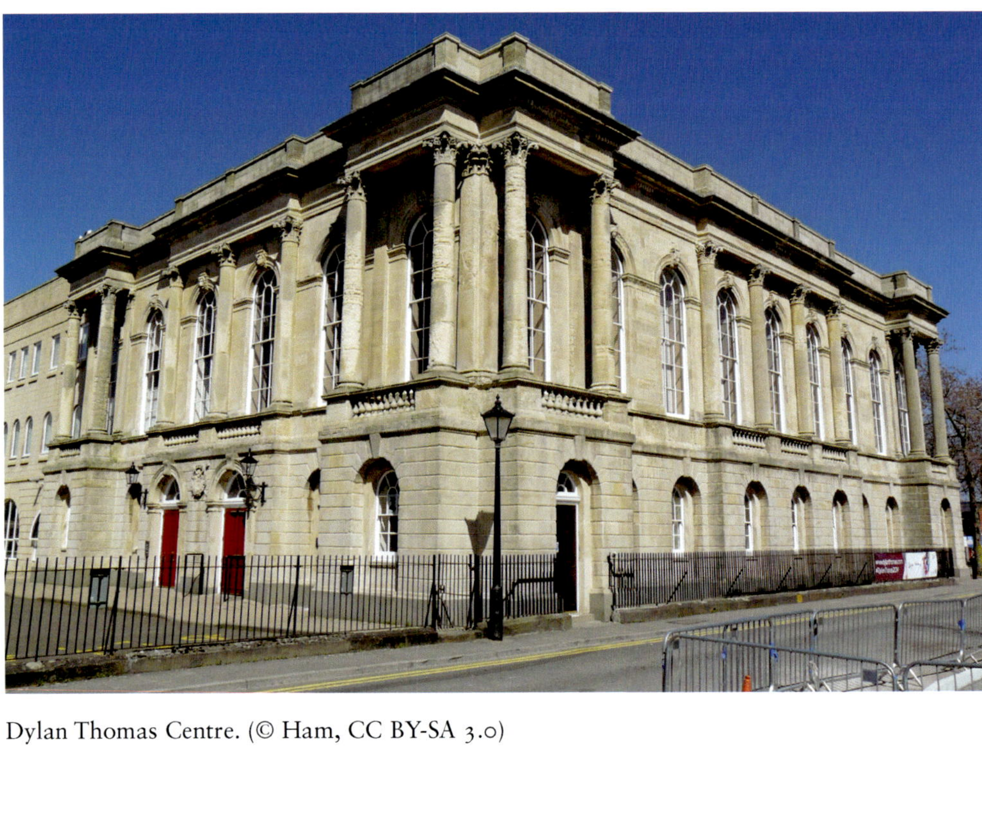

Dylan Thomas Centre. (© Ham, CC BY-SA 3.0)

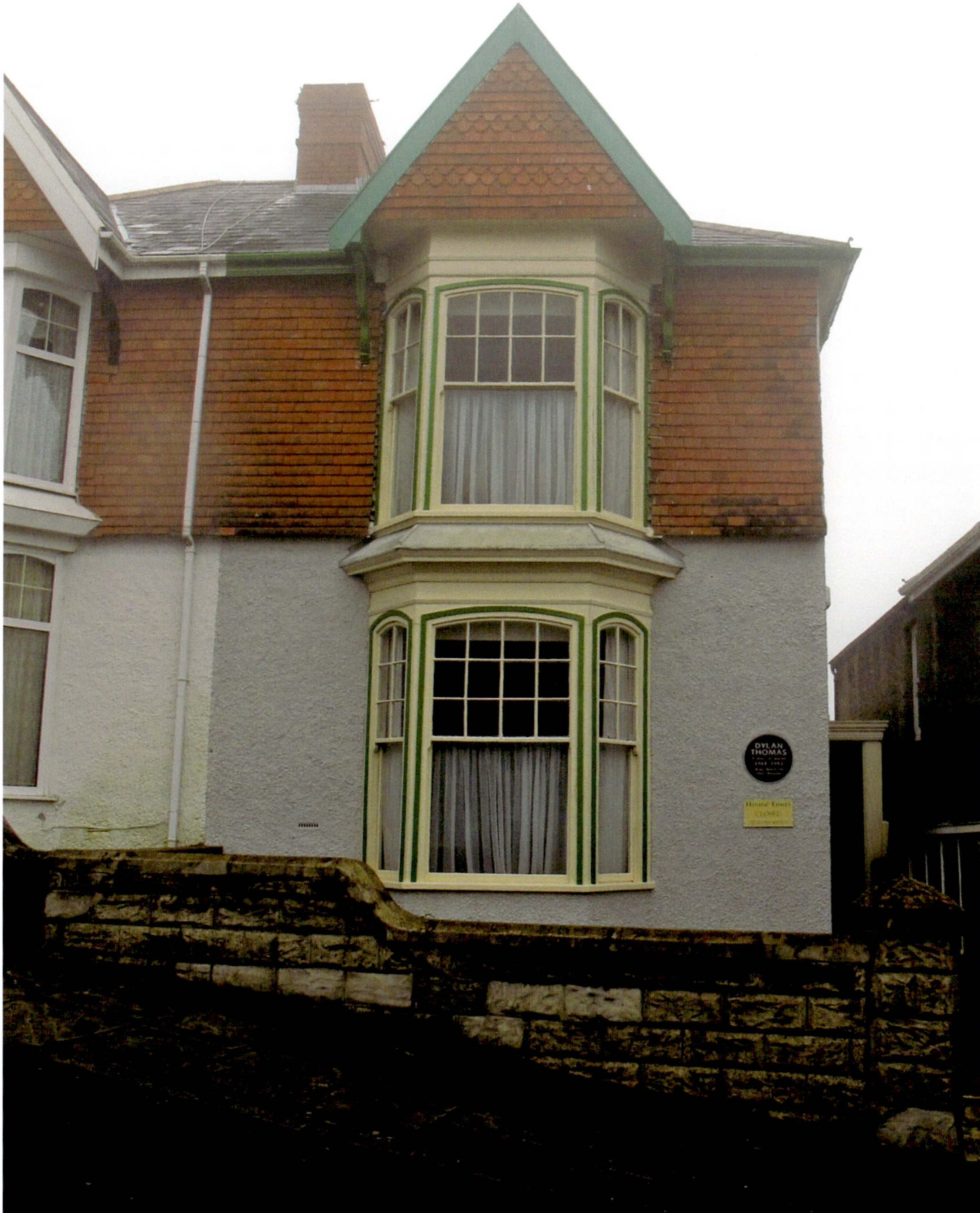

Dylan Thomas Birthplace, 5 Cwmdonkin Drive.

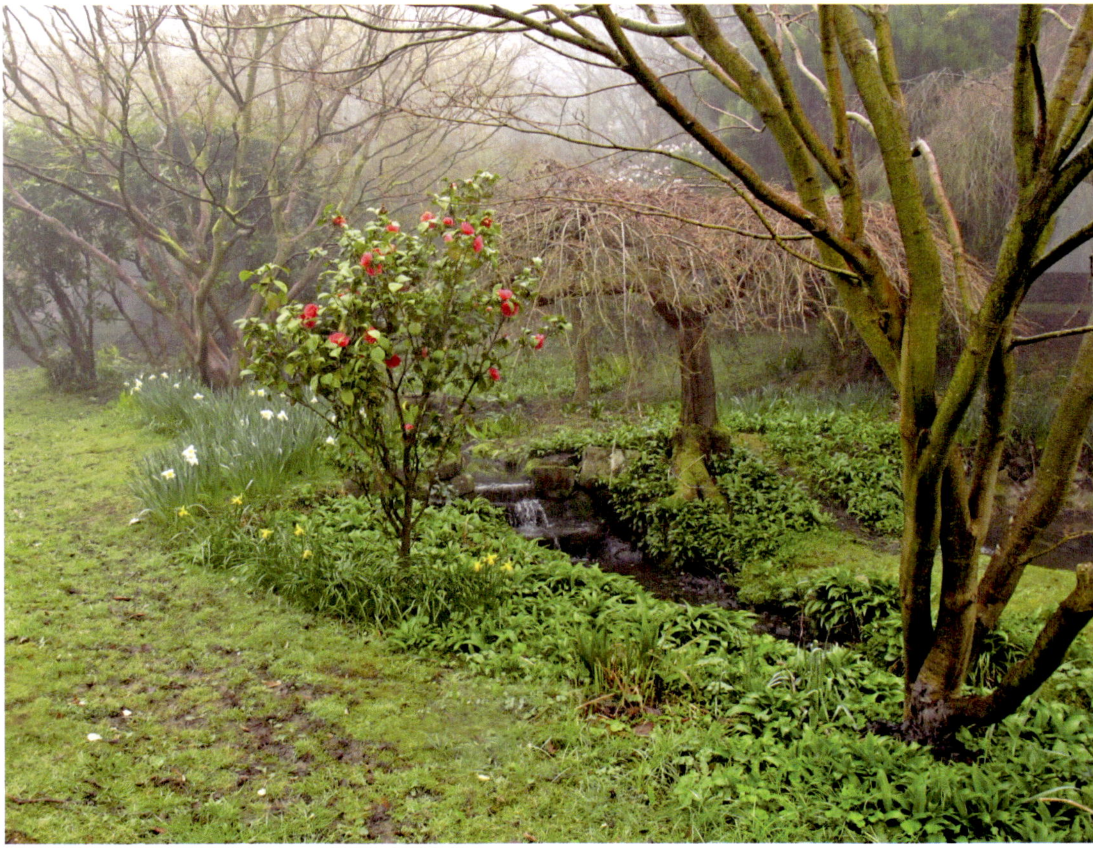

A foggy day by the stream in Cwmdonkin Drive.

Dylan's birthplace and family home at 5 Cwmdonkin Drive in Uplands is a popular pilgrimage destination for fans from around the world, and it was in 1939 during a return journey to visit his parents that Dylan met Margaret Thomas. They were mutual friends of a Mabel Davis, and following a chance encounter in Singleton Park, headed back to Davis's bedsit. That would be Margaret's only meeting with Dylan and she left Swansea herself soon after, but during a return visit of her own in 1973 she spent hours each day reading the paper in Cwmdonkin Park. It was early one evening as she sat at the foot of a slope overlooking the stream that she was suddenly struck by missiles. Small stones, branches, turf, and twigs pelted her from all directions, and being totally alone in the park save for the gardener who was some distance away, she assumed some mischievous boys had crept up on her. She walked up through the trees to investigate but was surprised to find she was very much alone. She shouted to the gardener to ask is he'd seen anything, who replied that he hadn't, and that nobody could have entered the park without him knowing. It was only when she sat back down that she suddenly thought of Dylan, that 'mischievous' boy whose childhood bedroom had overlooked the park. Further, she recalled how he had even written a poem about such a scenario, 'The Hunchback in the Park', in which youngsters threw stones from what might have been the very same spot. She assumed there must be a rational explanation, and yet she could not think of one.

Another person lucky enough to meet Dylan was a young man who would become one of Britain's most celebrated ghost hunters and president of the Ghost Club. Peter Underwood was working in the publishing industry for Dent in London at the time when the poet visited his office looking for an advance. Underwood recalled how, despite having never met before, Dylan wasted no time in asking him if he'd buy him a drink and, being an admirer, Underwood agreed. He asked Dylan to autograph his book and arranged to meet him for a pint in Charing Cross Road. The conversation naturally drifted towards the supernatural, and Underwood discovered that Dylan was 'by no means sceptical of the idea of ghosts'. When pressed on the subject he 'became very serious and said he had seen his father after his death, and occasionally he felt the unmistakable presence of his dead father'. He believed that ghosts were people not yet ready to move on and instead 'fought against death and refused to accept it'. As a result, 'something' lingered on after the demise of the physical body. In Dylan's most well-known poem, he urges his father, who is losing his sight at the end of his life, not to accept the inevitable and to keep on fighting. The words he uses have become his most famous lines, and they also appear to reflect his belief in an afterlife. That if we deny death with every fibre of our being, then we might, just might, walk this earth a little longer. Or to put it more poetically:

Do not go gentle into that good night.
Rage, rage against the dying of the light.

Bibliography

Barber, Chris, *Ghosts of Wales* (John Jones, 1979)

Books, J. A., *Ghosts & Legends of Wales* (Jarrold Colour Publications, 1987)

Evans-Wentz, W. Y., *The Fairy-Faith in Celtic Countries* (Oxford University Press, 1911)

Ferris, Paul, *Gower in History* (Amranaleg Books, 2009)

Gascoigne, Russell, *The Haunting of Glamorgan and Gwent* (Gwasg Carreg Gwalch, 1993)

Jones, Edmund, *The Appearance of Evil: Apparitions of Spirits in Wales* (University of Wales Press, 2003)

Lockley, Steve, *Ghosts of South Wales* (Countryside Books, 1996)

Newman, John, *The Buildings of Wales: Glamorgan* (Penguin Books, 1995)

Parsons, Ian, *Swansea's Grand* (Bryngold Books, 2010)

Radford, Ken, *Tales of South Wales* (Skilton & Shaw, 1979)

Rees, Mark, *Ghosts of Wales: Accounts from the Victorian Archives* (The History Press, 2017)

Rees, Mark, *Paranormal Wales* (Amberley Publishing, 2020)

Rhys, Ernest, *The South Wales Coast from Chepstow to Aberystwyth* (T. Fisher Unwin, 1911)

Sikes, Wirt, *British Goblins* (EP Publishing Limited, 1973)

Underwood, Peter, *Ghosts of Wales* (C. Davies (Publishers) Ltd, 1978)

Underwood, Peter, *No Common Task: The Autobiography of a Ghost-Hunter* (Harrap, 1983)

Vaughan-Thomas, Wynford, *Portrait of Gower* (Robert Hale Ltd, 1976)

Wilkins, Charles, *Tales and Sketches of Wales* (Daniel Owen and Company, 1879)

Other resources:
1940sswansea.co.uk
bbc.co.uk
coflein.gov.uk
Derek Acorah's Ghost Towns (Ruggie Media, 2006)
Fortean Times (I Feel Good Publishing, 2001)
Llyfrgell Genedlaethol Cymru/The National Library of Wales
ITV Cymru/Wales Archive at National Library Wales
Journal of the Society for Psychical Research
museum.wales
nationaltrust.org.uk
walesonline.com
South Wales Evening Post
spr.ac.uk

Acknowledgements

A huge *diolch o galon* to my family for their continued support, and to Nick Grant and all at Amberley Publishing for commissioning the book you now hold in your hands. *Paranormal Swansea* would not have been possible without the many ghost hunters and folklorists who treaded a similar path before me, the investigators and witnesses kind enough to share their time and experiences, and the fantastic photographers who are credited throughout. I would also like to thank: Steve Balsamo, Chris Carra, Ant Jones, Ronnie Kerswell-O'Hara, Rod Lloyd, Gayle Marsh, Karl Morgan, Mal Pope, Jenny White, The Comix Shoppe, Cymru Paranormal, The Rusty Cauldron, and you, dear reader, for daring to pick up this terrifying tome.

About the Author

For more than fifteen years, Mark Rees has published articles about the arts in some of Wales's best-selling newspapers and magazines. His roles have included arts editor and what's on editor for the *South Wales Evening Post*, *Carmarthen Journal*, *Llanelli Star* and *Swansea Life*. He has written a number of books, with those of a supernatural nature including *Ghosts of Wales: Accounts from the Victorian Archives* (2017), *The A-Z of Curious Wales* (2019), *Paranormal Wales* (2020), and *Paranormal Cardiff* (2023). In 2017 he launched the now annual 'Ghosts of Wales – Live!' event and in 2018 *Phantoms*, a play based on his ghost stories, was adapted for the stage by Fluellen Theatre Group.

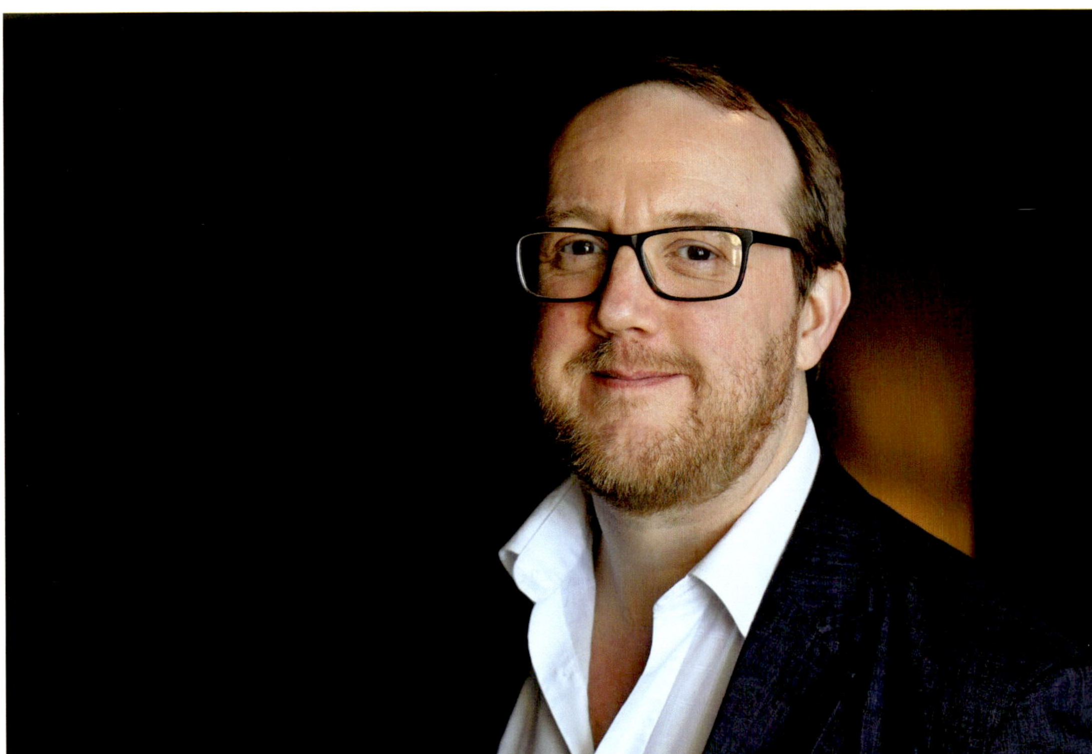

Mark Rees. (Photo by Gayle Marsh)